Nlp

The Essential Guide to Neuron Linguistic Programming

(How to Structure Success and Create Influence at the Expert Level)

Louis Nesmith

Published By **Bella Frost**

Louis Nesmith

All Rights Reserved

Nlp: The Essential Guide to Neuron Linguistic Programming (How to Structure Success and Create Influence at the Expert Level)

ISBN 978-1-7777786-3-7

No part of this guidebook shall be reproduced in any form without permission in writing from the publisher except in the case of brief quotations embodied in critical articles or reviews.

Legal & Disclaimer

The information contained in this book is not designed to replace or take the place of any form of medicine or professional medical advice. The information in this book has been provided for educational & entertainment purposes only.

The information contained in this book has been compiled from sources deemed reliable, and it is accurate to the best of the Author's knowledge; however, the Author cannot guarantee its accuracy and validity and cannot be held liable for any errors or omissions. Changes are periodically made to this book. You must consult your doctor or get professional medical advice before using any of the suggested remedies, techniques, or information in this book.

Upon using the information contained in this book, you agree to hold harmless the Author from and against any damages, costs, and expenses, including any legal fees potentially resulting from the application of any of the information provided by this guide. This disclaimer applies to any damages or injury caused by the use and application, whether directly or indirectly, of any advice or information presented, whether for breach of contract, tort, negligence, personal injury, criminal intent, or under any other cause of action.

You agree to accept all risks of using the information presented inside this book. You need to consult a professional medical practitioner in order to ensure you are both able and healthy enough to participate in this program.

Table Of Contents

Chapter 1: What Is NLP? 1

Chapter 2: The Power of Neuro-Linguistic Programming 14

Chapter 3: The NLP Techniques 29

Chapter 4: Applying NLP in Communication and Relationships................................... 42

Chapter 5: Limiting Beliefs and Self-Sabotage.. 55

Chapter 6: NLP in Business and Leadership 69

Chapter 7: Strategies Timeline Therapy for Personal Transformation 83

Chapter 8: Ethical Considerations in NLP Practice... 97

Chapter 9: What Is NLP? 111

Chapter 10: What Is The Level Of Education?.. 134

Chapter 11: What's A Representation? 148

Chapter 12: What Are The Predicates? 165

Chapter 1: What Is NLP?

Neuro-Linguistic Programming or NLP is an effective and transformational method of personal growth and communication that is increasing in popularity over the last few time. The program offers effective techniques that help us understand and altering the way we feel, think and behave, ultimately leading to greater productivity and success in professional as well as personal lives.

The premise of NLP is founded on the notion that thinking, words and behavior are connected and are able to be utilized to effect positive changes. Through understanding and applying the basic patterns that humans experience, NLP enables individuals to alter their thinking patterns and attain the goals they desire.

NLP is a collection of strategies that are able to boost various aspects of our lives, such as the health of your career, relationships as well as personal development. The techniques vary from basic activities to more complicated techniques, each created to assist people in gaining control over their thoughts emotional states, and behavior.

One of the main tenets of NLP is understanding that every person perceives reality differently. Every person is unique. Individual map of reality formed by their own memories, beliefs, and personal values. NLP helps us to acknowledge and accept these different perspectives and allows us to connect more effectively with people around us and strengthen our connections.

Through the use of NLP methods, people can conquer their fears, release negative feelings, and create powerful thinking habits. They can achieve their goals more easily and effectiveness, which leads to greater confidence and more success.

NLP isn't just a toolkit but a way to live your life. It can help individuals be accountable for their thinking or feelings and their actions and allows them to create significant changes to their lives. It encourages self-awareness, the ability to change, and personal growth and helps people become the very best version of them.

To sum up, in , NLP is a revolutionary and effective method for individual development and communication. It gives people useful tools and strategies to rewire their brains and attain their goals. It doesn't matter if you want to enhance your relationships, boost your professional career or improve your self-esteem, NLP has something to provide anyone. Take a look at the realm of NLP and uncover the secrets for a more satisfying and prosperous life.

The History and Evolution of NLP

The History and Evolution of NLP

Neuro-Linguistic Programming, commonly known as NLP is an effective method that has transformed the domains of personal development communications, therapy, and communication. It's a tool that is versatile that is beneficial for everyone regardless of experience or background. To fully appreciate and comprehend NLP It is vital to study its intriguing background and development.

The origins of NLP are traced back to the 70s, when Richard Bandler, a computer scientist, as well as John Grinder, a linguist began a mission to investigate the extraordinary talents of well-known therapists like Virginia Satir and Milton Erickson. Bandler and Grinder sought to unravel the methods and strategies that helped make the therapists they studied so efficient. Based on their research and observation they came up with the basic concepts of NLP.

The beginnings of NLP were filled with the discovery of strategies that would effectively modify behavior and improve communication. Bandler and Grinder found that by knowing the connection between mind (neuro) as well as the language (linguistic) as well as behavior (programming) the individuals can alter their lives, and attain their goals faster.

As time passed, NLP expanded its reach beyond the realm of therapy and communication. It developed into a method that can be used to a variety of settings, such as educational, business in sports, personal growth. The method gained acclaim because of its capacity to bring about lasting changes by changing your subconscious mind, encouraging self-awareness and increasing interpersonal relations.

Since its beginning, NLP has continually evolved and changed to accommodate the evolving needs of users and its wider audience. A variety of new techniques and approaches have been developed, adding to the vast array of NLP techniques. Beginning with Swish Pattern through Anchoring Technique to Anchoring Technique, each technique is designed for a specific use and can be customized to meet individual preferences and objectives.

Presently, NLP is widely regarded as an approach to change which empowers people to conquer difficulties, challenge the limitations of their beliefs and reach their maximum potential. Its efficacy has been confirmed through numerous success stories of individuals from all fields of study.

In it is clear that the development and development of NLP has been characterized by the constant pursuit of studying the human mind and maximizing the human capacity. Beginning with its humble beginnings during the 1970s, until its present status as a well-known method NLP has had a profound influence on professional and personal advancement. Through embracing the fundamentals and methods of NLP people from all backgrounds can gain access to the wisdom of the neuro-linguistic program and harness the power of their brains for the development of their lives and for success.

Understanding the Principles of NLP

Understanding the Principles of NLP

Neuro-Linguistic Programming (NLP) is powerful instrument that has the potential to dramatically alter the way we perceive, talk and reach our goals. In this section we'll explore the underlying principles of NLP and look at the ways they can be utilized to various areas of our daily lives.

The principle that drives NLP is the fact that the body and mind interact and continuously affect one another. The way we think, feel behavior, and thoughts are all connected, and through understanding this relationship, we are able to come up with strategies to alter our habits and obtain the desired results. NLP can help us effectively connect with our subconscious mind, which is responsible for our habits and automatic reactions and creates positive changes.

A further principle that is important to NLP is the idea that all of us are unique in our maps around the globe. Our beliefs, experiences and beliefs determine our views of reality and NLP assists us in understanding and accept the differences of each person. Through developing trust and gaining an understanding of others' viewpoints it is possible to improve the quality of our relationships both personally as well as professionally.

NLP additionally emphasizes the importance of language as well as its influence on our thinking and behavior. With the help of specific and effective pattern of language, we are able to be more effective in communicating and be a positive influence on others. NLP is a way of paying attentively to the words that we employ in our daily lives and also externally. We also make conscious choices that reflect the goals we have set and our ideals.

One of the fundamental tenets of NLP is the ability to take lessons from the best. When we study successful people and imitating their techniques to replicate their success for ourselves. NLP can help us identify and reproduce the thinking patterns as well as the behaviors and attitudes of people who are successful, which allows us to boost our individual growth and achievement.

In the end, NLP emphasizes the importance of adaptability and flexibility. Being open to other views and methods and perspectives, we are able to broaden our possibilities and discover innovative solutions to problems. NLP encourages us to accept the process of change as an opportunity to grow and growth.

In understanding the fundamentals of NLP is essential to unlock the mysteries of neuro-linguistic programming. Through recognizing the interconnectedness between our body and mind while recognizing the individuality of each and harnessing the potential of languages studying from success and fostering flexibility we are able to unlock our maximum potential and see remarkable outcomes across all aspects of our lives. If you're looking for improvement in your relationships, personal development or a career that is successful, NLP offers invaluable tools and strategies that will allow you to live your ideal life.

How NLP Can Transform Your Life

How NLP Can Transform Your Life

Neuro-Linguistic Programming (NLP) is an effective tool with potential to change your life in many ways. For those who are looking for improvement in your relationships, personal growth or improved communication and even success in your career, NLP offers a comprehensive method to aid you in reaching your objectives.

In its essence, NLP examines the connection between the thoughts we think, our language and our behavior. In understanding and exploiting the connection between these three, we can change our perspectives, override barriers, and achieve positive changes.

One of the major advantages of NLP is the ability to change negative assumptions. Many times, we're restricted by barriers that we create ourselves as well as negative thinking patterns which hinder advancement. NLP gives strategies and methods to recognize and change the beliefs that limit us, and allow our minds to be empowered which support personal development.

In addition, NLP equips us with efficient communication abilities. In understanding the communication patterns as well as non-verbal clues from others to become powerful, persuasive, and empathic communicaters. Being able to better connect with other people not only enhances the quality of our relationships, but it creates new opportunities within our professional and private life.

A different aspect that is transformative of NLP is its emphasis on the role of modeling the highest level of excellence. NLP professionals study successful people and study their methods, attitudes, and actions to duplicate the success they have achieved. In interpreting the behavior patterns from these roles models we will be able to speed up our growth and reach the same results in various fields of life.

Furthermore, NLP offers powerful techniques for personal growth and control of emotions. By using techniques like meditation, anchoring, or reframing, it is possible to achieve control of the emotions we experience, overcome anxieties and fears as well as create a optimistic, resilient mental state. It allows us to face the challenges of life with a sense of confidence, strength and an increased awareness of ourselves.

Whatever your experience or goals, NLP has something to give to anyone. No matter if you're a college professional, student as a parent or a business owner NLP's principles and practices of NLP can enrich your life in positive ways.

Chapter 2: The Power of Neuro-Linguistic Programming

The connection between Mind and the Language

Within the vast world of neuroscience-based programming (NLP) the most important element that is of immense importance is the relationship between mind and the language. How we speak does not just reflect our thinking and opinions, but it also has significant impact on our brain functioning and general well-being. Knowing this relationship can help unlock the mysteries of NLP and help us change our lives.

Language is a potent instrument that can shape our lives. The words we use as well as the manner in which we communicate with us can impact our attitudes, thoughts as well as our emotions and behavior. In observing the patterns of our speech and patterns, we can gain a better understanding of the subconscious mind of our brain and are able to alter it to produce the desired results. NLP gives methods for harnessing your language's power which allows us to effectively communicate with others and ourselves.

Our brains are always processing data from outside which is why language serves as the link between our inner thoughts and our external surroundings. Through enhancing our language skills and abilities, we will be able to improve the ability of communicating our ideas and desires effectively, resulting in better connections and more satisfaction in different areas of our lives.

The relation between language and the mind goes far way beyond just language. Words we speak with shape our worldview. In particular, words that are negative can perpetuate negative thoughts and reduce our capacity. Conversely utilising positive and motivating words can help us rewire our brains to help us achieve our goals and grow personally.

NLP provides a variety of methods to redefine our language patterns and harness the potential of our minds. Techniques like reframing anchoring, and modelling assist us to understand the structures of language that are at the root of our lives and allow us to create positive change.

In gaining a better understanding of the relationship between the mind and the language it is possible to discover the secrets of NLP and experience personal change. NLP allows us to alter our minds, unwind from the limitations of our beliefs and open up new possibilities for us. NLP allows us to speak effectively, develop connections with others and create positive changes.

No matter if you're a beginner or a seasoned practitioner learning to understand the relationship between the mind and the language is vital to harness the potential of NLP. Through incorporating NLP methods into your daily routine it will allow you to unlock the secrets of NLP and unlock your full potential.

In that the relationship between the mind and the language is the most fundamental element of Neuro-linguistic programming. In recognizing the power behind language and the way it affects our emotions, thoughts and behaviours We can leverage the power of language to improve our lives. NLP offers methods to alter our brains, to communicate effectively and experience the personal development we desire. Whatever your experience or passions, understanding the relationship between your brain and language is vital to unlock the mysteries of NLP and unlocking your full potential.

The Role of Neurology in NLP

The Role of Neurology in NLP

Neuro-linguistic Programming (NLP) is an extremely effective method that could aid individuals in improving their communication abilities, boost their personal growth, and meet their goals. In the underlying principles of NLP is the ability to understand how the neurology of our brain influences the way we think, behave and feelings. In this chapter, we'll look at the importance of neurology within NLP and the ways that knowing the inner workings of our brains can help uncover the mysteries of NLP to everyone.

The term "neurology" refers to the study of nervous systems which includes the brain as well as the intricate functions it performs. Our neurology is the way which we experience the world around us, make sense of information and react to stimuli from outside. NLP acknowledges the significance in understanding the complexity of this system in order to maximize the potential of personal development and change.

The fundamental principle behind NLP is that the neurology of our brain cannot be fixed. It is possible to be altered. Through understanding how the brain process information and develops behaviors We can recognize and alter unhelpful patterns changing them to more efficient ones. This information allows us to manage our feelings, thoughts and behaviors, which can lead to the success of our professional and personal lives.

The neurology plays an important function in the language aspects of NLP. The way we use language is a key component of our neurology as it is a reflection of our inner thought process and affects our external interactions. Through observing and analysing our language patterns, NLP practitioners can gain insight into the beliefs that underlie our behavior as well as our values and motivations. The knowledge gained allows them to implement effective solutions to help those with limitations to achieve the desired results.

Additionally, the neurology system is connected to sensory sensations. NLP recognises that we see the world around us through the senses of sight tasting, hearing, touch and smell. When we understand how our brain handles sensory input it is possible to improve our capacity to communicate and interact with other people. NLP methods like anchoring and reframing make use of our experiences with sensory information to form positive connections and change the negative feelings and behavior.

As a summary, neurology is a fundamental component of NLP and is the keys to unlocking its secrets for all. When we understand how the brain operates, we can modify our brains to attain the personal development we desire, increase our the communication abilities, and achieve the goals we set for ourselves. NLP allows individuals to gain control of their thinking as well as their emotions and behaviors and lead an improved and more satisfying life. If you're beginning to learn about NLP or a seasoned practitioner, gaining a deeper understanding of the neurology role will enhance your understanding and increase the effectiveness using the potential of NLP.

Linguistics and Language Patterns in NLP

Linguistics and Language Patterns in NLP

Language is the most fundamental instrument that we employ to express thoughts, express emotions and establish relations with one another. In the world of neuro-linguistic programming (NLP) Language plays an essential role in the understanding of our behavior. When we study the intricate nature of linguistics as well as language patterns, we are able to unlock the mysteries of NLP and improve our abilities to communicate for both professional and personal success.

Linguistics is the study of language, is the foundation of NLP. It focuses on the structure, sound, and the meaning behind language which allows us to comprehend how individuals encode their experience by using words. Through understanding the patterns of language that we are able to discern the meaning behind someone's phrases and gain a better comprehension of their thinking and motives.

In NLP the term "language patterns" refers to the patterns of recurring structure and words people employ in order to communicate. In recognizing these patterns we can access the subconscious mind to affect behaviour more efficiently. By using, for instance, specific language patterns, such as presuppositions or commands embedded in the language can subtlely influence the thinking of someone without anyone noticing it. The patterns help us convey more effectively, create trust, and get the goals.

A powerful pattern of linguistics employed to aid in NLP is known as "The Meta Model." It is comprised of a series of questions which help discover and confront the limits within our thinking. Through the use of this Meta Model, we can assist individuals to expand their perspective and overcome their limiting beliefs and grow personally. This model allows us to delve further into someone's mind and discover the root of their thoughts and patterns.

An additional element of linguistics NLP is studying languages that are a reflection of the person's personal perception. These patterns, referred to as "submodalities," involve the aspects of sensory perception that include auditory, visual and kinesthetic components. When we understand and utilize submodalities, it is possible to modify our internal perceptions of reality and alter the way in which we see the world around us which ultimately leads to behavior shifts and improvements in outcomes.

In the study of linguistics and language patterns are fundamental to the study of Neuro-Linguistic Programming. In knowing the structures and patterns of the language we will be able to unravel the mysteries of our human behaviour and communications. If you're a professional seeking to improve your influence capabilities or are a student wanting to grow personally, dipping into the field of language and patterns of NLP can offer you powerful methods to unleash the potential of your brain and help you achieve success throughout your entire the world.

In the hyper-connected world that we live in, achieving it can be difficult to achieve success. There is always a desire for our dreams however, something keeps us from achieving our goals. What if the secret to success is in our minds? The chapter, "Programming Your Mind for Success," investigates the benefits of Neuro-Linguistic

Programming (NLP) and its ability to help anyone reach their maximum potential and reach their fullest.

Understanding NLP:

Neuro-Linguistic programming is an effective method of personal growth and allows individuals to rewire their brains to be successful. In understanding the intricate link between our brain's neurological functions along with language and behavioral patterns, it is possible to take control of our thoughts as well as our emotions and behavior.

Shaping Your Belief System:

One of the most fundamental tenets of NLP is the conviction that the thoughts and beliefs we hold determine our life. Through identifying and changing negative beliefs, we can change our mindsets to be convinced of our achievement. This chapter explores a variety of NLP methods, like anchoring and reframing that help people transform their the negative thoughts into positive ones.

Harnessing the Power of Language:

The role of language plays an important part in our communication with each other and ourselves. With NLP it is possible to learn how to utilize the language patterns that influence the way we think and feel. The chapter discusses the art of powerful language. This includes the use of affirmations self-talk, and visualization techniques to train our minds to be successful.

Developing Powerful Habits:

The success of a person is usually the consequence of a consistent approach. In order to achieve remarkable outcomes, it is essential to establish powerful patterns that will help achieve the goals we set. This chapter explores the ways NLP techniques can be applied to develop new habits and break patterns and help develop a successful approach. From observing successful people and creating individualized success routines and strategies, we will find the methods and techniques to train our brains to ensure the long term achievement.

Overcoming Challenges and Building Resilience:

The path to success is not without difficulties and obstacles and. This chapter highlights the ways NLP provides us with techniques to face difficulties, increase resilience and remain positive regardless of hardship. In programming our minds to think of obstacles as opportunities to grow, we are able to transform setbacks into steps toward achievement.

"Programming Your Mind for Success" is a chapter in the book that examines the transformative potential that is Neuro-Linguistic Programming in unlocking the strategies to achieve the success you desire.

Through understanding the relationship between our thinking, belief system and our actions it is possible to reprogram our brains to be more aligned with our objectives and goals. No matter if you're an entrepreneur, student or someone seeking to unleash their potential, this chapter provides important insights and strategies which can be utilized by anyone, regardless of qualifications or previous experience. Utilize the potential of NLP and get started on your path to a more fulfilling and rewarding life.

Chapter 3: The NLP Techniques

The process of setting goals is an important aspect of both professional and personal achievement. It helps us stay focused, motivated and clarity for the actions we take. Yet, many individuals are struggling to set goals that inspire and help them achieve their goals. In this chapter we'll look at how to set clear and convincing goals with Neuro-linguistic Programming (NLP) methods.

The neuro-linguistic programming technique is a potent method that blends the sciences of linguistics and psychology with behaviour patterns to aid people achieve their objectives. One of the main tenets of NLP is the notion that language and thoughts determine our worldview. In harnessing the power the subconscious mind, by aligning our thoughts and our language to the goals we have and goals, we are able to create the right path for achievement.

For setting clear and compelling targets, it's essential to recognize the importance of focusing. Ambiguity or vague goals lack definition and therefore are less likely to achieve. Focus on establishing objectives that are precise and measurable, achievable as well as time-bound (SMART). If you set your objectives with precision you give your brain a an objective that you can work toward.

Additionally, it's important that your goals are compelling. An effective goal is one that inspires and stimulates the person who is pursuing it on a deeper degree. It should be in alignment with your ideals, beliefs and aspirations. If you can connect your goals to the core values of your life and building an emotional connection with them you boost the intensity and determination to reaching your goals.

In this section it will teach you various NLP methods to increase the efficiency of the goal-setting method. They are based on affirmation, visualization and anchoring. Visualization is the process of creating vivid and clear visual images of your ideal result, allowing you to build a conviction and confidence. Affirmations are affirmations that can help you achieve your goals and assist you to break through self-limiting thoughts. Anchoring refers to the association of a certain physical or mental condition with the goals you want to achieve, and allowing you to gain the motivation you need and keep your focus when needed.

If you apply these NLP methods and including them into your goal-setting procedure, you can discover the maximum potential of your brain and get amazing outcomes. Whatever you're seeking, whether professional advancement, personal development or improved interpersonal relationships, making clear and credible goals with NLP will help you to achieve the lifestyle you want. Begin to realize your full potential and make the dreams you have in your head with the effectiveness of NLP and goal-setting.

Anchoring: Harnessing States of Excellence

Anchoring: Harnessing States of Excellence

The vast world that is Neuro-Linguistic Programing (NLP) it is possible to use an effective technique called anchoring. It allows us to access our internal capabilities and attain the state of perfection, which allows us to accomplish our objectives and lead a fulfilled life. Anchoring is a powerful instrument that is able to be utilized by any person, irrespective of background or previous expertise with NLP.

But, what is anchoring? In essence, anchoring is the act of linking an internal reaction or state with any external trigger or stimuli. By consciously connecting a positive emotion that is characterized by enthusiasm or confidence with a certain psychological or physical trigger it is possible to get to the state anytime we want. Anchoring gives us an effective and stable way to gain access to powerful states, which allows us to achieve success in all areas of our life.

Imagine being able to quickly access a sense of clarity and peace during an emotional situation, or to summon the confidence to make an impressive speech. When you anchor, it's not just possible, but simple. Through the deliberate anchoring of positive state of mind, we will establish a solid path towards excellence, which makes it much easier to reach the goals we set and over come the obstacles.

Anchoring is a process that is comprised of three actions: establishing the desired state, finding the anchor and creating connections between these two. It could involve recollecting an experience or memory where you experienced the desired state vividly and clearly in a way, then relating the state to a particular phrase, gesture, or mental picture. As you time, your anchor will become connected to the state you want which allows you to reach anytime.

Anchoring can be utilized in different areas of our lives, such as personal development as well as relationships and professional advancement. Through anchoring certain states, such as the ability to feel motivated, confident or relaxation, we will boost our performance, increase the quality of our communications and establish stronger bonds with other people. In addition, it can assist people overcome their fears as well as negative feelings, which allows us to overcome internal barriers to unlock the full potential of us.

In it is an extremely effective method in the field of Neuro-Linguistic Programming. It lets us draw on our internal reserves and access high-performance states, making it simpler to reach the goals we set and lead an enjoyable life. Through the conscious anchoring of positive emotions with specific triggers that we are able to easily gain access to these states of abundance whenever they are needed. Anchoring is an instrument which is available to anyone regardless of the knowledge or background in NLP The tool can change our lives in massive ways. Therefore, why put off? Get started harnessing your anchoring power right now to unlock your full potential.

Reframing: Shifting Perspectives and Beliefs

Reframing: Shifting Perspectives and Beliefs

Within the field of Neuro-Linguistic Programming (NLP) reframing is an effective technique that permits people to change their perspective and assumptions, leading to personal development and change. If you're looking to get rid of limiting beliefs and improve your relationships or boost your overall health reframing is an effective tool open to anyone.

Fundamentally, reframing is changing how we think about and view things, situations or events. Our beliefs and views are shaped through our experiences in the past and experiences, which may often hinder our growth and hinder our growth. By consciously rethinking our beliefs and thoughts and perspectives, we are able to break free of these limitations and set to new opportunities.

One of the most fundamental tenets of reframing is to recognize the multiple viewpoints for any circumstance. Whatever we think of as an issue or challenge could have the potential to be the potential for a beneficial lesson or chance to grow. When we reframe our perception to shift our attention from the issue toward the solution. We can empower ourselves to discover innovative and efficient ways to conquer difficulties.

Reframing can also mean asking questions and challenging existing assumptions. Most of the time, we believe in convictions that do not serve our needs or are based on a lack of knowledge. If we look at these beliefs as well as considering other perspectives to expand our perspectives and become to a new way of thinking.

Reframing also allows you to alter our perception of things and events. Instead of dwelling upon past errors or mistakes and failures, we are able to frame these as opportunities to learn from them. When we see setbacks as an opportunity to improve our performance and overcoming obstacles, we will be able to build the ability to bounce back and keep optimism.

In relational contexts the ability to reframe can be especially beneficial in the context of relationships. Through reframing the way we perceive the actions and behaviors of others it can help us improve the understanding, empathy as well as our communication abilities. A shift in perception can help us build healthier and more fulfilling interactions with people around us.

In Reframing can be an transformative technique within the domain of Neuro-Linguistic Programming that is accessible for everyone. When we shift our perceptions and perceptions, we will be able to overcome limits, face challenges and unleash our full potential. If you're looking for improvement in your relationships, personal development or simply an improved outlook on the world, reframing your perspective could be an effective strategy to use in your quest towards self-discovery, and personal the empowerment.

Excellence in Modeling: Learn from the best

The Model of Excellence: Learning from the Top

In the field of neuro-linguistic programming (NLP) one of the most effective methods is modeling success. The concept is based on learning and imitating the actions of strategies, mindset, and tactics of people who have had extraordinary results in their particular field. In understanding the pattern of success that these people exhibit We can then learn how to imitate their successes within our lives.

The subchapter focuses on the amazing possibilities of demonstrating excellence in our lives and the ways it can be utilized in various areas of life. If you're looking for improvement in your personal life, success at work or better relationships this notion can change the game.

The initial step to modeling excellence is to determine the those who have produced remarkable results in your chosen area. They could be famous sportsmen, leaders, entrepreneurs and even everyday people who have achieved amazing accomplishments. When we study their behaviors as well as their beliefs and methods, we get valuable insight into the factors that set individuals apart from others.

When we've found the models that are our best After identifying our models of excellence, we begin the strategies and methods they employ. The process involves looking at their behavior as well as listening to their personal stories and identifying the fundamental pattern that is the reason for their accomplishments. In this way it is possible to implement these practices in our lives, and begin getting closer to our goals.

The art of modeling excellence doesn't mean trying to imitate someone else's behavior. It's about knowing the underlying principles that drive the success of others and adjusting the same to our own unique situation. When we integrate these ideas in our beliefs systems and routines, we will be able to make our own way towards excellence.

Through this chapter in this chapter, you'll find real-life examples of those who have successfully mastered how to model success. They range from successful entrepreneurs who established successful companies to people who have faced significant obstacles Their stories will motivate and inspire you to realize your potential.

No matter if you're brand novice to NLP or an expert practitioner Modeling excellence could transform your lifestyle. Learning from the top experts, we are able to access our endless possibilities and be able to achieve remarkable. Come along in this journey of discovery to discover the secrets of excelling in modeling within the exciting realm of Neuro-Linguistic programming.

Keep in mind that the ability to achieve greatness is within you.

Chapter 4: Applying NLP in Communication and Relationships

Effective Rapport Building

The ability to build rapport is a key ability in the field of neuro-linguistic programming (NLP) that has the potential to have an enormous impact on interpersonal and professional interactions. If you're an therapist, salesperson or a teacher, or just someone looking to develop their communication abilities knowing how to master creating rapport is crucial.

Then, what is rapport? In NLP it's the strong bond and trust created between two people. This is the condition of balance wherein people recognize and appreciate their perspectives. This leads to effective cooperation and communication. The ability to build rapport lets you build a positive impact to influence others and establish lasting connections.

One of the most important aspects for building rapport is being able to recognize and reflect the non-verbal signals of the person you're in contact with. These non-verbal cues can be found in gestures such as gesturing, facial expressions and voice tone. Through observing and imitating these signs, you'll be able to make a feeling of comfort and familiarity and make the person you are talking to feel respected and valued.

A key aspect to creating rapport is listening actively. Instead of waiting for you to be the next person speaking, you should give your complete focus to the individual in the room in front of you. Engage with them in the words they speak, ask them clarifying questions and offer compassionate answers. When you truly listen to them, you will be able to establish connections on a deeper one, which will help build confidence and trust.

Additionally, the usage of language plays an essential part in building rapport. Be aware of the language, words, phrases and metaphors your partner utilizes, and then incorporate the same into your speech. The linguistic match helps to build a sense of knowledge and understanding. It also helps in improving the relationship between the two of you.

It's also crucial to know and take control of your own emotional state when you interact with others. People are drawn by people who radiate optimism, confidence and compassion. When you develop these qualities in your own self, you will be able to influence the mood of those around you and help build more harmonious connection.

Effective relationships are the mainstay of NLP which helps us communicate to others at a more intimate degree. In synchronizing and reflecting the non-verbal signals, listening actively and using the language correctly and regulating our own mental state and emotions, we can create strong and meaningful connections. In both professional and personal situations mastering the art of building rapport is a great way to improve abilities to communicate, influence and overall health.

The Power of Language and Verbal Communication

The Power of Language and Verbal Communication

Language is among the most effective tools we have at our at our disposal. Through language can we convey our thoughts, emotions as well as our desires and wants. Language is the means by which we communicate to others, establish relationships, and communicate details. Within the field of neuro-linguistic programming (NLP) knowing that the importance of words as well as spoken communication is vital for growth in one's personal life and effective communicating.

NLP helps us understand that words we speak influence the way we think, feel as well as our behavior. Language we use could either help us or hinder our abilities. When we are aware of our patterns in language it is possible to take control of our thinking and make positive changes within our lives.

Have you noticed that certain words and phrases immediately trigger a powerful emotional reaction? It is due to the fact that the brains of humans are wired to identify certain feelings and meanings with certain phrases and words. As an example that the term "love" may evoke feelings of happiness and warmth, and"fear" could trigger feelings of anxiety and joy "fear" may trigger anxiety and fear. Through understanding the power behind words, we are able to use words to affect our feelings and trigger positive emotions.

The way we communicate is not just dependent on the words we use however, it is also about how we say these messages. The tone we use, the pitch that we choose, and body language communicate meaning, and they can significantly affect the efficacy of the communication we use. When we are aware of the non-verbal signals and body language, we will increase our capacity to communicate with other people and communicate the message with greater effectiveness.

In the world of NLP There are a variety of methods and techniques that aid us in harnessing our ability to harness the powers of language as well as spoken communication. As an example, reframing is a method which involves altering our perception of and communicate about a particular scenario. When we reframing our words it is possible to shift our mindset and result in better outcomes.

A further powerful method that is utilized in NLP is using storytelling and metaphors. Metaphors help us communicate complex concepts in a clear and comprehensible manner, which makes it easier for people to comprehend and to remember. When we incorporate storytelling into the way we communicate, we will engage our audiences and build an even deeper bond.

In it is evident that the value of communication through language can't be understated. When we understand the power of our words, and employing efficient communication strategies will allow us to improve our own personal development and build more lasting relationships and have greater success across all aspects of our lives. If you're a professional or a student or just someone who is who is interested in developing their own personal skills learning the art of speaking and communication is a crucial ability that will change your life.

Non-Verbal Communication and Body Language

Non-Verbal Communication and Body Language

When it comes to communication the use of words is only just a small portion of the information being transmitted. The body language, also known as non-verbal communication, plays a crucial part in the daily interaction. Knowing this part of communication is vital for those who want to increase their knowledge of Neuro-linguistic programming (NLP).

Non-verbal communication is comprised of a myriad of components that include facial expressions, poses, gestures and even the sound of the voice. Like words, which can be utilized to convey information and convey meaning, the body can also convey emotions, intents and even attitude. In recognizing and decoding these non-verbal signals that we receive, we gain greater understanding of ourselves as well as other people.

One of the fundamental tenets of NLP is that the way we think and feel are inextricably linked to the physical conditions we are in. The way we sit, for instance is a significant factor in our mood. If we adopt a calm and healthy posture, we immediately feel more confident and confident. However the slouched, closed off posture may cause feeling of anxiety and a lower self-esteem.

In addition, being aware of the subtle signals of other people helps us build relationships and strengthen our connections. The body language that we mirror of the person we're communicating with may create a feeling of trust and familiarity. Also, the ability to detect subtle signals of disagreement or discomfort in the body language of another individual lets us adjust the way we communicate and adjust the way we communicate.

Understanding the body language of others can help in finding out if someone is deceiving. The way that people move their bodies, face expressions and changes in voice tone may indicate that people are being untruthful or omitting the truth. As we improve our abilities in watching these indicators to become proficient in discerning truth, and make informed choices.

In the next sections, we'll dive deeper into the complexities of non-verbal communication as well as body language. We will look at the many kinds of body language, and facial expressions as well as their significance. Additionally, we will learn strategies for improving our body language, and increasing our ability to discern the subtle signals of other people.

It doesn't matter if you're a professional who wants to increase your negotiation abilities or a therapist looking to build stronger relationships to your clients, or just somebody who's seeking to comprehend human behavior in a deeper way learning the technique of non-verbal communication as well as body language is sure to prove valuable in the intriguing world of neuroscience-based programming.

NLP in Conflict Resolution and Negotiation

NLP in Conflict Resolution and Negotiation

Conflict is a natural aspect of human life, regardless of whether it's in our private relations, work environments and even inside ourselves. Yet, how you approach conflict and manage conflicts could make a big distinction in the outcomes that we get. Neuro-Linguistic Programming (NLP) provides effective tools and strategies which can be used in negotiations and conflict resolution in order to assist individuals to find common ground, and reach wins for everyone.

NLP stresses the importance of language and communication in shaping our beliefs as well as our experience. Through understanding and using our ability to use language it is possible to effectively handle conflicts and use them as possibilities for learning and growth. When it comes to the resolution of conflicts, NLP techniques enable us to identify and modify the negative communication patterns, making it possible to have more constructive and constructive interactions.

One of the main tenets of NLP is that each person has distinct model of reality. That means that every person experiences and interprets conflict differently according to their personal knowledge and experiences. When we recognize and accept these different perspectives, we will be able to deal with conflicts with empathy and compassion, which can create an environment that is more collaborative.

NLP methods also give useful insights into communication that is non-verbal that plays an important part in conflict resolution as well as negotiation. When we observe and understand facial expressions, body language and tonality it is possible to gain more insight into the core emotional and psychological factors that cause the conflict. The knowledge gained lets us adjust the way we communicate and react in a manner which promotes understanding between people and a resolution.

In negotiations, NLP techniques can be especially advantageous. Through the use of language patterns, such as leading and pacing, we are able to build rapport with the opposing party, and build an atmosphere of trust and co-operation. NLP can also help us focus on the words spoken by other parties and help us discover the deep needs and wants of each party. With this information and understanding, we can create mutually beneficial solutions that serve the needs of everyone in the process.

Chapter 5: Limiting Beliefs and Self-Sabotage

On the road to your personal development and improvement One of the main challenges we face is the limiting beliefs we hold about ourselves and self-defeating behaviors. The negative habits we have can stop us from reaching the fullest potential of ourselves and leading an enjoyable life. However, thanks to the methods and tools of Neuro-Linguistic Programming (NLP), it is possible to break free of the limitations of our lives and bring about permanent transformation.

Limiting beliefs refer to the ideas and assumptions we make concerning ourselves, our fellow humans as well as our environment that block our growth. They are usually developed during our childhood, or through negative past experiences. They function as filters that we use to perceive and understand the world and influence our thinking as well as our emotions and behavior. Yet, these beliefs cannot be fixed in the stone. When we know how they're created and applying NLP methods, we are able to transform them into affirming beliefs that align with our aspirations and goals.

Self-sabotage is a common obstacle which hinders our progress and the success we desire. This is the attitude that we perform which undermines our progress and targets. If it's self-doubt or procrastination or fear of failure Self-sabotage holds us within a loop of negative thoughts and hinders our from taking the needed actions towards the desired results. NLP offers effective methods to recognize and defeat self-sabotaging behavior and allow the individual to let go of the destructive habits and make progress in confidence.

One of the fundamental principles of NLP is understanding that language, thoughts and behaviour are all interlinked. When we alter one aspect one thing, we influence surrounding elements to create positive change. By using different NLP techniques like reframing, visualisation, and anchoring, we are able to change our thinking patterns and generate different patterns of thought, emotion and acting that match with our dreams and goals.

In this chapter in which we'll look at methods and exercises that can be used to defeat limiting beliefs and self-sabotage. In this chapter, we will explore the potential of re-frame negative perceptions, employing strategies for visualization to build an exciting future and using anchoring techniques to gain access to powerful state of mind. When used consistently and in a deliberate manner are able to help anybody regardless of their past or present situation, get rid of the limiting belief systems and self-sabotaging behavior.

It's important to keep in mind that breaking through limiting beliefs as well as self-defeating is a continuous process. While we continue to develop and grow and develop, new obstacles may emerge while old habits could be rediscovered. With the skills and knowledge of NLP We have the ability to overcome the obstacles to create an existence that is full of purpose satisfaction, happiness, and achievement.

Discover the secrets to Neuro-Linguistic Programming and unleash your maximum potential. Take advantage of the power of overcoming negative self-sabotage and beliefs that limit you, and begin a transformational process to improve your personal life and achievement. The possibilities are unlimited.

Building Confidence and Self-Esteem

Building Confidence and Self-Esteem

Self-confidence and confidence are the key elements of happiness and success across all facets of life. If you want to be a success in your profession and build relationships that are satisfying, or just lead an enjoyable life, gaining confidence and self-esteem is crucial. In this chapter we'll explore the ways in which Neuro-Linguistic Programming (NLP) can aid you in identifying the key for building self-confidence and confidence.

NLP provides a variety of strategies and techniques which can help individuals alter their beliefs and mindsets regarding their own self. Through understanding the power of language as well as its impact on our feelings and thoughts It is possible to change the way you talk about yourself to replace it with positive, empowering words. With the help of affirmations as well as visualization exercises, NLP enables you to alter your thinking to be confident in your talents and abilities.

Furthermore, NLP provides tools to aid you in identifying and transforming the beliefs that are restricting you. Through identifying the subconscious beliefs which undermine confidence and self-esteem can confront them and change them to empowering convictions that will help your progress and achievement. NLP techniques like reframing and anchoring can assist you in changing your perception and build a more optimistic and positive self-image.

A key aspect to building confidence and self-esteem is the development of efficient communications capabilities. NLP helps you to employ the language of non-verbal communication to create relationships, inspire others and speak confidently and with confidence. When you master the art of communicating effectively and enhancing your relationships, have an impact that is positive on other people and increase your confidence in yourself.

Apart from the ability to communicate and speak, NLP offers techniques to control and conquer anxiety and fear. Through techniques like The Swish Pattern or the Fast Phobia Cure, you will be able to eliminate your the irrational fear and develop an understanding of the emotions. When you overcome the fears you have, confidence and self-esteem increase naturally.

In the end, NLP emphasizes the importance having clear objectives and committing to a consistent approach to achieve them. Through defining your objectives and break them down into smaller steps and gaining momentum, you will be able to increase your confidence and boost confidence of your capabilities. NLP techniques such as those used by the New Behavior Generator can help to create behavior patterns and new routines that are in line with your goals and boost self-confidence as well as confidence.

In Building confidence and self-confidence is an essential aspect for your personal development and achievement. By applying the concepts and methods of NLP it is possible to unlock the potential of your mind and change the way you think.

Utilizing the power of language, changing limitations, enhancing communications skills, conquering anxiety and fear as well as setting clear goals that will give you unshakeable confidence and self-confidence that will allow you to excel to succeed in every aspect of your living. Get started on your path to self-confidence and self-esteem today. learn the secrets of Neuro-Linguistic Programming to help you achieve development and achievement.

Managing Stress and Emotional Well-Being

Managing Stress and Emotional Well-Being

In our fast-paced society Stress has become a normal aspect of life. From pressure at work to personal struggles We are continuously bombarded by stressors which can cause a lot of damage to our mental health. But, through the use of Neuro-Linguistic Programing (NLP) We can develop effective methods to handle anxiety and improve our psychological wellbeing.

NLP is a potent technique that allows people to recognize the connections between their language, thoughts and behaviour. Utilizing NLP techniques, we will be able to change our thinking and develop an optimistic mindset which allows us to better deal with anxiety.

One of the most fundamental tenets in NLP is the realization that the emotions we experience and our thoughts are tightly connected. Thoughts that are negative can trigger negative emotions that may in turn lead to stress levels rising. When we practice positive self-talk and changing negative thoughts into positive ones, you can change your perspective and lessen anxiety.

A different powerful NLP method for managing tension is the technique of anchoring. Anchoring is the act of linking a certain trigger, for example, an object or word, to an emotion, like peace or calm. When we create an anchor that is positive that allows us to quickly reach the state of well-being anytime we require it, even when we are in an emotional stressor.

Furthermore, NLP offers effective strategies to manage emotions. Through becoming conscious of our patterns of emotional behavior and the assumptions that motivate our emotions, we are able to take control of the emotions we experience and select more positive actions. Methods like the Swish pattern or the Circle of Excellence can help to break free of negativity and develop an optimistic and productive outlook.

Additionally, NLP provides tools for creating resilience and increasing the quality of life for people. With techniques such as timeline therapy as well as parts integration it is possible to heal the scars of old wounds, shed negative emotions and create an emotional foundation that will ensure peace and stability.

In controlling anxiety and stress is an essential aspect of our lives. Neuro-Linguistic Programming offers a wealth of methods and strategies that help us achieve this goal. When we practice NLP methods, we are able to alter our mindset, manage the emotions we experience, and increase our the capacity to endure, which leads to a healthier and fulfilled life. No matter if you're seeking improvement in your personal life, professional growth or just a greater awareness of your mind, NLP can unlock the ways to manage stress while improving your mental health.

Enhancing Creativity and Problem-Solving Skills

Enhancing Creativity and Problem-Solving Skills

The ability to think creatively and solve problems is crucial to personal and professional performance. If you're an entrepreneur, artist as well as a scholar or someone who is looking to grow personally, building these capabilities are essential. In this section this chapter, we'll look at how Neuro-Linguistic Programming (NLP) can reveal the secret to increasing the ability to think critically and solve problems to everyone.

NLP provides a range of methods and strategies which can assist individuals in tapping the creative side of them. One of these techniques is reframing. Reframing is the process of changing the view or perspective of an event and can result in innovative solutions. When we shift our focus, and examining a situation in a variety of angles and perspectives, we are able to uncover new perspectives and concepts.

Another effective tool used to use in NLP involves modeling. Modelling is the process of studying and imitating the thinking and behavior of individuals who have succeeded within a specific field. In observing and implementing the methods of problem-solvers who are creative and innovators, we will be able to improve the capabilities of our team to create new ideas.

Additionally, NLP emphasizes the power of communication and language in stimulating creativity. Through the use of specific linguistic patterns that allow us to rewire our thinking patterns, and improve our thinking capabilities. By utilizing NLP techniques like the use of metaphorical language as well as shifting language concepts, we can create a more flexible and innovative mental state.

Alongside linguistic strategies, NLP also utilizes visualization methods to boost imagination. When we visualize our desired outcome vividly and engaging our entire senses, we are able to stimulate our imagination and create creative concepts. The exercises of visualization assist us to overcome mental obstacles to create connections and increase our creativity.

In the end, NLP encourages individuals to be open to new ideas and accept failure as an opportunity to grow. If we adopt a method that is constantly learning and experimenting and experimenting, we will develop the capacity to be creative and build the ability to solve problems effectively. NLP can help us view the challenges as an opportunity to move towards achievement and urges us to adopt a growth-oriented mindset.

In Neuro-Linguistic Programming provides numerous techniques and methods to increase the ability to think and solve problems that are suitable for all. Utilizing reframing, modelling language patterns, visualization as well as adopting a growing mentality, people can unleash their creativity and build efficient problem solving skills.

Chapter 6: NLP in Business and Leadership

NLP Techniques for Effective Leadership

A strong leadership ability in every field that is professional or personal, or even within a larger community. Neuro-Linguistic Programming (NLP) offers an array of methods which can significantly enhance capabilities as a leader. Through understanding and applying NLP methods, people will become more powerful convincing, effective, and efficient leader. This chapter will discuss important NLP methods that allow managers to unleash their best qualities as well as their team members.

A powerful NLP method is the art of building relationships. People who have a trust with their employees build trust and respect, encouraging cooperation and open communication. NLP can provide a range of methods to build rapport with your team members by using mirrors to reflect body language or matching tone, as well as employing similar patterns of language. Utilizing these strategies leadership can create an intimate connection with their teams, making it simpler to encourage, motivate and inspire and help them achieve shared targets.

Another crucial NLP method for effective leadership is to use words patterns. Language patterns can have an impact on how other people perceive us and respond to our actions. People who can master the art of language precision are able to affect and motivate their employees better. NLP provides techniques such as reframing that help leaders to frame issues as opportunities and also presuppositions that subtly incorporate suggestions into their communications. Through the use of these communication patterns, leaders are able to change the mental and behavioral habits of their teams, which leads to greater performance and improvement.

In addition, NLP techniques can help executives develop a clear idea and establish high-quality objectives. Through techniques like"the "Disney Strategy" or the "Well-Formed Outcome Model," leaders are able to clarify their goals as well as develop a comprehensive program of action, and encourage their staff to produce amazing outcomes. They can help leaders bring their teams together to achieve an agreed-upon vision and create an understanding of the purpose behind their work and participation.

Additionally, NLP can enhance a leaders' emotional intelligence and allow the leader to comprehend and control the emotions of their own and their colleagues. Through the use of techniques like"the "Anchoring Technique" or the "Swish Pattern," leaders are able to control their mood, remain at peace under stress and effectively respond to difficult scenarios. The ability to master their emotions allows managers to be able to act with empathy as they resolve conflicts and create a harmonious workplace.

For , NLP techniques offer powerful tools for leadership effectiveness. Through mastering the art of building rapport, the use of language patterns, goal setting as well as emotional intelligence leaders can motivate and inspire their teams to produce remarkable outcomes. These methods are useful to any leader in any area or field, and provide the framework to allow for professional and personal growth. When you understand the power of NLP you can make anyone more effective and successful leader. This will have an effective impact on the individuals as well as organizations.

Influencing and Persuasion Skills in Business

Influencing and Persuasion Skills in Business

In today's highly competitive and fast-paced business environment, having the ability to influence and persuade effectively is essential to succeed. No matter if you're manager, salesperson or an entrepreneur, your capability to influence and convince people can greatly impact the growth of your career and accomplishments. This subchapter outlines the powerful methods and the principles in neuro-linguistic programming (NLP) that will help you improve your persuasion and influence skills within the realm of business.

Neuro-linguistic programming is an evolving method that blends psychological principles, language patterns and strategies for communication to assist individuals in understanding and harness the intricate relationships between language, the mind and the way we behave. Through the application of NLP techniques, you will get a better knowledge of how humans consider, take decisions and react to various ways of communicating.

One of the primary elements of persuasion and influence is to build rapport with people. NLP can provide a range of techniques for creating a powerful relationship and build trust. These include such things by mirroring body language the use of tonality that matches, as well as making use of similar language patterns. Utilizing these methods to make a welcoming and comfortable atmosphere for efficient communication, helping you to share your thoughts and impact others positively.

A second essential business skill is the ability to speak persuasively. NLP offers tools that can improve the patterns of your speech and language that allow you to express your ideas and thoughts better. When you understand the many ways people manage information (visual and auditory) You can adapt your language style to fit the way they prefer to communicate, making it easier to influence the audience in a positive way.

In addition, NLP offers techniques to overpower resistance and objections.

Through developing your sense of acuity and being aware of subtle signals, it is possible to determine the primary issues or concerns someone might be facing and respond to them in a proactive manner. This is especially beneficial in negotiations and sales scenarios where knowing how to respond to objections could be the difference between a successful or unsuccessful deal.

Persuasion and influence abilities aren't about manipulation or coercion, but rather they're about understanding people and establishing mutually beneficial relationships as well as achieving win-win outcomes. NLP provides you with methods to effectively influence and convince, enabling you to build collaboration, inspire teams and reach the goals of your company.

If you're a veteran professional or are just beginning your professional career mastering the art of influence and convincing can greatly increase your efficiency and effectiveness. Through studying the fundamentals of neuro-linguistic programming and infusing the techniques of neuro-linguistic programming into your communication arsenal, you will be able to unlock the techniques to become an effective and influential person in business.

NLP for Sales and Marketing Success

NLP for Sales and Marketing Success

In the current business environment Effective methods for marketing and sales is essential to achieve successful business. In this chapter we'll look at how Neuro-Linguistic Programming (NLP) can prove to be an effective tool that can improve your marketing and sales strategies.

NLP A method of study that studies the interplay between the language of a person, their patterns of behaviour, as well as subjective experiences It can give valuable insights to understand and influence the thoughts of your customers. Utilizing NLP methods, you will be able to gain a better comprehension of the target market as well as communicate better, and eventually drive greater performance in marketing and sales.

One of the most important principle of NLP is building rapport. The ability to build rapport is vital to establish trust and a connection with your customers. This is the basis of every successful marketing or sales venture. Utilizing NLP techniques like the mirroring process and match, you will be able to subtilly sync your body speech, tone of voice and the patterns of your language to your clients, thereby providing a feeling of comfort and confidence that will impact their purchase choices.

In addition, NLP can help you get valuable insight into your customer's needs and motives. Utilizing techniques like sensors and calibration you are able to observe and understand the non-verbal messages and gestures of your customers, making it possible to discern the preferences of your clients and adapt your marketing and sales messages to suit. A personalized approach to marketing will not help your clients feel valued and appreciated and appreciated, but will also improve the efficacy of your sales and marketing strategies.

NLP provides effective persuasion strategies that could dramatically impact business's sales and marketing performance. Through understanding and using the language patterns that are used, like presuppositions and commands embedded in the language that you are able to influence the customers' thoughts, making them more likely to make positive buying choices. Furthermore, NLP techniques like reframing helps you to transform objections or obstacles into opportunities, helping you overcome obstacles and conclude deals with greater efficiency.

Then, , NLP can be an important factor when it comes to the success of marketing and sales. Through understanding and applying the fundamentals and strategies of NLP it is possible to build relationships, understand the needs of your clients, and influence them in a more effective manner. No matter if you're an expert in sales, marketing or business owner including NLP in the marketing and sales strategies you employ will help you get amazing performance. Therefore, take a dive into the realm of NLP and discover the secrets of selling and marketing success.

Enhancing Communication in the Workplace

Enhancing Communication in the Workplace

Communication is the heart of any productive workplace. This is the base on that collaboration, understanding and efficiency are based. In this chapter, we'll look at how Neuro-Linguistic Programming (NLP) can reveal the secret to improving collaboration at work, benefitting everyone who is involved.

NLP is a distinctive method of better understanding and improving communication paying attention to the interactions between language, the mind and the way we behave. Utilizing NLP techniques, users will gain an understanding of their communication habits and be able to modify the way they communicate to improve their outcomes.

The most important aspect of NLP is its recognition of the fact that different individuals process information in various ways. Through understanding and adjusting to this difference, communication could be more efficient. In particular, certain people have a preference for visual communication, while some prefer to use auditory or kinesthetic methods of communicating. If we can tailor our language and presentation to suit these needs it is possible to ensure that the messages we send are recognized and comprehended more effectively.

Another important tool of NLP is the capacity to create relationships. When we establish a relationship to others, we can create the environment for respect and openness. This is achieved by the use of mirroring techniques and matching which allow us to mimic the body language of another person and tone of voice or even the words we use. It creates a feeling of connection and can help build a greater degree of understanding.

NLP further emphasizes the importance of listening with a sense. When we are actively listening to other people it is possible to gain information about their opinions as well as their needs and worries. It allows us to react in a more appropriate and compassionate manner creating better connections and cooperation in the workplace.

In addition, NLP techniques can be employed to break down barriers to communicating, including confusions, or conflict. Utilizing reframing methods people can change their mindset and come up with innovative ways of dealing with difficult scenarios. This will result in positive and constructive conversations which allows groups to function more effectively.

In improving communication within the workplace is vital for all employees, irrespective what their position or job. Incorporating NLP methods in our communications practices We can discover the secrets of more productive and productive interactions. If it's learning about different ways of communicating, establishing trust, active listening or even overcoming obstacles, NLP provides a valuable instrument to enhance communications in the workplace.

Chapter 7: Strategies Timeline Therapy for Personal Transformation

Within the broad field of neuro-linguistic programming (NLP) it is possible to find an effective technique called Timeline Therapy. This chapter aims to provide a better understanding of this amazing technique and how it can enable personal transformation for anyone.

In its essence, Timeline Therapy recognizes the profound link between the way we view time and the emotions we experience. It recognizes that the past memories shape the reality we live in today and impact the future. Through understanding and modifying our timelines, we are able to successfully release negative emotions as well as overcome the limitations of our beliefs and build a positive future.

The initial step of Timeline Therapy is to access the personal timeline of our lives, which is an imaginary representation of the current, past as well as the future. Through imagining ourselves in this timeline we learn more about how previous experiences have affected our attitudes behavior, attitudes, and feelings. The self-awareness of oneself is the starting point to change.

When we've found the root of unhelpful beliefs or negative feelings and negative emotions, we are able to employ different methods to let them go. By using the technique of dissociation and visualization it is possible to dissociate our self from the past and see them through an entirely different angle. Dissociation lets us release any baggage from our past that might hold us back.

Timeline Therapy also empowers us to redefine our experiences from the past. Reliving significant moments as well as incorporating new knowledge and knowledge, we are able to interpret our experiences to see them in a more positive, stimulating perspective. Reframing our perceptions frees our minds from negative feelings that are associated with these experiences that can hinder personal development and change.

Alongside healing the past injuries, Timeline Therapy offers a unique chance to design an exciting future. When we imagine ourselves in the future and imagining the outcomes we want to achieve We can bring the subconscious with our goals and desires. The alignment speeds up the fulfillment of our desires, leading to a happier and purpose-driven existence.

If we're looking to grow personally as well as emotional healing or a greater level of success, Timeline Therapy has the ability to bring about change for all. Through harnessing the potential of our personal timelines it is possible to free ourselves from the burdens of our past, alter our perceptions, and create our future in accordance with our most cherished goals.

To sum up, in , Timeline Therapy is an extremely effective technique within the field of Neuro-Linguistic Programming. It provides a unique chance to personal growth by exploring the link between our experience of time as well as our feelings. By using techniques like reframing, visualization, and setting goals, Timeline Therapy enables individuals to shed negative emotions as well as overcome the limitations of their beliefs and build a positive future. If you're looking to heal from past traumas or personal challenges or improve your performance, Timeline Therapy has the ability to reveal the secrets of transformation for everyone.

Hypnosis and NLP Integration

Hypnosis and NLP Integration

Neuro-Linguistic Programming (NLP) is an extremely effective technique which can help discover the secrets of your mind to achieve the success you desire in your professional and personal life. When it is used in conjunction with the art of hypnosis NLP is even more effective. This chapter focuses on the interaction of hypnosis with NLP and provides insight on the way these two strategies are able to work in tandem to bring about long-lasting transformation.

The practice of hypnosis is long-standing acknowledged as an effective instrument to tap into unconscious mind. Inducing a state of trance it allows people to connect with their internal sources, break through their convictions, and implement beneficial changes to their lives. However, NLP provides a framework to understand the way that language and behavior affect our thinking and behavior. Combining these two methods to enhance the efficacy of each.

A way that both hypnosis as well as NLP can work together is by using the hypnotic patterns of language. NLP practitioners have a knack for making use of language to influence and influence others. And when coupled with hypnotic ideas it can make the effect far more powerful. With carefully selected terms and phrases, we are able to bypass our conscious minds and reach the subconscious creating lasting, profound changes.

Another method by the way these methods could be used together is by anchoring. NLP helps us to make anchors that are triggers that induce a desired mood or a feeling. Incorporating hypnosis into the procedure, we are able to deepen the anchor's power and make it more powerful. By using the hypnotic process, we can induce an increased level of potential for suggestion, which allows people to react more strongly to the anchor and feel an immediate change.

In addition, hypnosis is utilized to increase the efficacy of NLP techniques like time therapy, or parts integration. Inducing a state of hypnosis the individual can access their emotions and memories more readily which allows for a deeper understanding and resolving past conflict or trauma. Hypnosis in combination with NLP helps speed up recovery process and encourage individual growth.

In the combination of hypnosis with NLP is an effective method to professional and personal growth. Through the combination of techniques from both hypnosis and NLP users can discover the mysteries of their mind, break through limitations and bring about lasting change. It doesn't matter if you're looking for the process of self-improvement or therapy, or just learning about the functioning of your mind, the integration of hypnosis as well as NLP can be a powerful solution for all.

Meta-Programs: Understanding Human Behavior Patterns

Meta-Programs: Understanding Human Behavior Patterns

The vastness of human behaviour there are patterns and trends which influence our thinking the way we feel, our actions, and emotions. These patterns, also called meta-programmes, offer valuable insight on how people think and interact with their surroundings. Knowing these patterns lies at the foundation of Neuro-Linguistic Programming (NLP), an effective tool to help you achieve personal transformation and growth.

Meta-programs are considered as operating systems for our brains. They serve as the filter that help us process information and come to the decisions. When we understand these patterns we will gain a better comprehension of our own and other and improve our communications, stronger relationships and a better personal growth.

In this section in this chapter, we'll explore the meta-programmes and the ways they impact our actions. Then, we will explore the many meta-programs which shape our thoughts, including the emphasis on potential versus constraints, the need to think big or pay focus on detail, and the desire to be driven with rewards or repercussions.

Furthermore, we'll discover the ways that meta-programmes affect our ways of communicating. A few people are more drawn toward others, with a focus on feelings as well as relationships. Others concentrate on work and facts. Recognizing these differentiators will help us to tailor the way we communicate to be better with other people regardless of whether they are in intimate interactions or in professional situations.

In recognizing and understanding the meta-programmings we create in ourselves and meta-programs, we will gain more awareness of ourselves and control the way we behave. It is possible to identify the behaviors that are no longer serving us, and then replace them with positive ones that are more powerful. As an example, if you tend to be prone to having an internal view, constantly considering our own wants and needs, we may be taught to broaden our perspective to take in the viewpoints of other people, resulting in better relationships.

This chapter will offer concrete exercises as well as techniques for working out and identifying meta-programs. With NLP methods, we will discover ways to change our meta-programs within ourselves and help others to do the same. Once we are conscious of these patterns, and understanding their effects it is possible to unlock the mysteries to Neuro-Linguistic Programming and unleash our maximum potential.

No matter if you're brand unfamiliar with NLP or are already familiar using it, this chapter will lead you through the world of meta-programs. This book will provide users with the necessary tools to comprehend human behaviour patterns and tap into their potential to personal transformation and growth.

Modeling Excellence: Strategies for Success

Modeling Excellence: Strategies for Success

In the field of Neuro-Linguistic Programing (NLP) One of the fundamental principles is that of modeling the highest level of excellence. This strategy is powerful and helps us discover the secrets of success through learning and imitating the methods and actions of people who have made it to the top within their fields of expertise. If you're an entrepreneur, student, professional, or someone seeking to improve themselves Understanding and applying the techniques for model high-quality can transform your life.

What makes modeling excellence important in Neuro-Linguistic Programming? It allows us to gain knowledge directly from the people who already have accomplished the skill we wish to acquire. Through observing their behavior as well as their language, habits of mind, ideas, and strategies it is possible to gain insights into their thinking process and reproduce their achievements for ourselves.

First step in modelling excellence is to find who or what group you would like to represent. It could be an accomplished businessperson, an acclaimed professional athlete, a gifted artist, or any other person that has reached a certain high level of proficiency within their area. When you've found your subject then the following step would be to research and analyse their actions as well as their language habits and their mindset.

If you pay attention You can begin to recognize the most effective methods and strategies that lead to their achievement. What is their everyday routine? What are their methods of communicating with other people? What are their convictions and values? Take note of the small details because they contain the key to their success.

After you've gathered sufficient information regarding your ideal model The next step is to incorporate the strategies they employ into your everyday life. The process involves adopting their principles and patterns of language, re-creating their models and implementing their methods. When you do this it is basically rewiring your brain to be in alignment with the best patterns.

It is crucial to remember that being an example of excellence does not mean just about imitating others blindly. It's about understanding the fundamental principles and methods that are responsible for their effectiveness and adjusting the strategies to suit your particular conditions. By doing this you are able to design your own pathway to success by leveraging the knowledge and experience of others that have gone before you.

In that, modeling excellence can be an effective strategy in Neuro-Linguistic programming that allows users to gain access to the secrets to the path to success. Through studying and replicating techniques and habits of the most successful people We can gain direct knowledge from their experience and speed up the pace of our own progress towards excellence. If you're an academic, professional or someone who is simply seeking improvement in your life, you should embrace the effectiveness of modeling excellence and discover your potential.

Chapter 8: Ethical Considerations in NLP Practice

The Importance of Ethical Standards in NLP

Neuro-Linguistic Programming (NLP) is an effective tool that could change the way people communicate, think and accomplish our objectives. The program offers strategies and methods that can improve our lives as well as increase our personal development. But, when it comes to the attainment of these rewards it is essential to be aware of the significance of ethical principles within NLP.

The ethical standards serve as a foundation for both users and practitioners of NLP to make sure that the methods and techniques are employed wisely and with the highest interests of the people who are involved. They are a fundamental rule to ensure honesty, respect and the fairness of. If we follow ethical guidelines that we will be able to tap into the full capabilities of NLP without inflicting harm or manipulating other people.

One of the most important ethics principles of NLP is the right to informed consent. It means that NLP practitioners must thoroughly explain their methods as well as the potential results as well as any risks that could be posed to participants and clients. A well-informed consent allows individuals to decide on their own regarding their involvement in NLP procedures. It makes sure that they're aware of potential consequences and provide their consent freely and without pressure or coercion.

It is also an important aspect of ethics when it comes to NLP. Practitioners need to have a clear knowledge of their personal boundaries, and make sure that they're not violated during NLP sessions. The ability to respect boundaries can foster confidence and provides a secure space for people to examine their feelings, thoughts and behavior.

Confidentiality is a further important ethical aspect for NLP. Participants and customers must feel assured that personal data and the experiences they share during NLP sessions will remain secret and will not be divulged without their agreement. Confidentiality builds confidence and allows people to reveal and dive into their inner world without fear of judgement or intrusion.

Alongside these basic ethics, NLP practitioners should continuously work towards personal development and awareness of themselves. It is about recognizing and confronting all biases, prejudices as well as personal limitations which might affect their work. Through this, professionals will ensure that their actions and actions are not influenced by any personal agendas and focus on the health and development of their clients.

In ethics are essential to the application of NLP. Through adherence to these guidelines, NLP practitioners as well as those who use NLP are able to ensure that strategies and methods are utilized in a responsible manner, while respecting limits and confidentiality. A moral NLP practices promote a secure and supportive environment that allows to personal development and growth. It is vital for anyone who is involved in the field of neuro-linguistic programming to accept and adhere to ethical principles to maximize the power of NLP.

Ensuring Consent and Responsibility in NLP

Ensuring Consent and Responsibility in NLP

Within the realm that is Neuro-Linguistic Programing (NLP) In the world of NLP, it's crucial to prioritize respect and consent. NLP methods have the potential to affect and alter individuals their lives. However, the power of NLP must be utilized ethically and with a sense of responsibility. This chapter is designed to highlight how important it is to ensure the consent of those who are using NLP methods.

Consent, within the context of NLP means the participation of individuals and their consent by individuals in any NLP procedure. It is essential to get an informed consent prior to making use of NLP methods for someone. Consent guarantees that the person is conscious of the intent as well as the potential results and the potential risks that could arise from the NLP procedure. In the absence of consent, NLP can become manipulative and un-moral. So, it's the responsibility of practitioners to respect the autonomy of individuals and get their permission prior to taking any action.

Furthermore, responsible behavior is a key element in NLP. As NLP professionals, we have an obligation of morality to apply our expertise and know-how in a responsible manner. That means that we must be mindful of the impact that our choices and words can impact the people around us.

Practitioners need to be sure that the intentions they express truly aim at being supportive and helping others, instead of manipulating or controlling their actions.

Being accountable also means accepting the limitations of NLP. Although NLP can be an effective instrument for personal development and transformation, it's not an all-encompassing solution. It is important to realize the fact that NLP methods are not suitable to everyone in every circumstance. Practitioners need to be transparent and clear about the positives and disadvantages of NLP and ensure that people can make informed decisions.

Additionally, NLP practitioners should be cognizant of ethical issues that are associated with NLP. That includes respecting confidentiality, observing boundaries within their professional environment, and avoiding from exploitation of weaknesses. NLP must be conducted by a professional with integrity, and aligned with ethical standards.

To guarantee consent and accountability for the practice of NLP Practitioners should focus on continuous education and self-reflection. Being aware of the most recent advances regarding NLP as well as regularly reviewing your own practice can assist keep ethical standards in place. Getting feedback and supervision from skilled practitioners may give valuable information and assure that you are accountable.

In the need to ensure the consent of both parties is essential when it comes to the application of NLP. In gaining permission, respecting the boundaries of their practice, and being responsible Practitioners can provide an environment that is safe and welcoming that allows individuals to experiment and gain of NLP methods. If they adhere to the ethical standards, NLP can truly unlock the mysteries of Neuro-Linguistic Programming to benefit everyone.

Handling Confidentiality and Privacy in NLP Practice

Handling Confidentiality and Privacy in NLP Practice

When it comes to the field of neuro-linguistic programming (NLP) professionals are charged with an immense responsibility for maintaining the confidentiality and security of their clients. This chapter is designed to provide clarity on how important it is to handle sensitive data and guaranteeing absolute privacy of everyone who participates in NLP practices.

Confidentiality is a cornerstone of any moral NLP procedure. It is the protection of private and sensitive information provided by clients during their sessions. Being an NLP practitioner, it's important to build a culture of trust, and to assure the clients that all information shared will be kept completely confidential. Confidentiality for clients is not just what establishes trust but also offers the right environment for people to discuss the thoughts, feelings and feelings with no fear of being judged.

To ensure privacy, NLP practitioners should adopt certain key methods. It is first and foremost important to seek an informed consent from the clients clearly defining the limits of confidentiality as well as the exemptions from this policy. It is essential to make sure that the client is informed of the circumstances under the event that confidentiality needs to be compromised or violated, for instance in situations that could cause immediate harm to oneself or other people.

Second, NLP practitioners must store the client's information in a secure manner. That includes using secure digital systems and locked cabinets for records that are physical. Additionally, practitioners must not discuss cases and sharing information about clients in any way outside of their therapeutic relationships, except when specifically authorized or legally mandated to disclose information.

Privacy On the other hand is more than just keeping confidential information. It covers the larger notion of respecting an individual's private boundaries as well as ensuring their security throughout NLP sessions. Practitioners should provide a safe and quiet environment with no interruptions or distractions. It allows patients to be fully engaged in the process and to feel safe talking about their experience.

Furthermore, NLP practitioners should emphasize the importance of privacy for their clients and assure them that their opinions, values and personal experiences will be protected throughout the process. Through creating an atmosphere which is private, individuals are able to explore their own inner world without restriction, which allows NLP methods to work better for personal development and change.

In managing privacy and confidentiality is of crucial importance in NLP practice. NLP practitioners have to build and keep trust by ensuring clients that personal data will remain private except for situations where there is a risk of harm. Privacy, which goes beyond privacy, means respecting your personal boundaries, and ensuring a safe and secure area for clients to talk about their ideas and experience. In adherence to these principles, NLP practitioners can create the conditions that encourage improvement, empowerment, and positive changes in their clientele.

Maintaining Professionalism and Integrity in NLP

Maintaining Professionalism and Integrity in NLP

When it comes to neuro-linguistic programming (NLP) keeping a high level of professional integrity and professionalism is vital. NLP is an effective instrument that could lead to change in professional and personal lives however, it should be managed with care and prudence. This chapter is designed to clarify the importance of professionalism and honesty in NLP as well as how it could positively impact professionals and those interested in this area.

Professionalism in NLP is a broad term that covers many elements, such as ethical behavior as well as continuous education and adhering to the established standards. Practitioners need to consider the health and the best interest of their clients by offering them a secure and a supportive space. It is about respecting their independence as well as their confidentiality and maintaining strict limits. Through adherence to professional ethics, NLP practitioners will build confidence with their clients building a solid therapeutic relationship which facilitates changes.

Integrity is a foundation on the foundation upon which professionalism within NLP is constructed. Practitioners should be transparent, honest and honest when they interact. They must refrain from offering false or false performance. Instead, they should concentrate on delivering accurate data and setting realistic expectations as well as providing useful information to their clients. Integrity not only increases the trustworthiness and credibility of NLP as a profession, however it also guarantees that the clients are provided with the top quality treatment.

Being professional and honest requires continuous self-development as well as studying. NLP is an evolving discipline that is constantly evolving professionals must keep current with the most recent methodologies, research findings, and most efficient techniques. In addition, by constantly expanding their expertise and understanding they can provide better and more efficient interventions based on evidence for their clients. In addition, continuous learning fosters an attitude of humbleness and curiosity, which allows professionals to evolve and adapt according to the constantly changing demands that their customers.

If you are looking to learn more about NLP Professionalism and honesty are the most important criteria to consider when looking for guidance or support. It is vital to choose a practitioner who is accredited skilled, knowledgeable, and dedicated to enforcing the highest standards of ethics. If you choose practitioners that are committed to honesty and professionalism, clients are able to ensure they get the best treatment and assistance throughout their own personal development and change.

Chapter 9: What Is NLP?

Neuro Linguistic Programming (NLP) is a constantly evolving practical framework and area of research that studies communication and behavior focused on understanding and exerting influence on interactions between our brain processes, linguistic behaviors, and the expressions we use.

NLP fundamentally lets people replicate the success strategies of those who have achieved success in their fields of expertise. If you're looking to become the top golfer on earth or a top sales rep, NLP will help you get there by sharing the secrets of the people who have achieved the highest levels of success. It is essentially, NLP helps you unlock their expertise and unlocking the potential you haven't realized.

The core of NLP can be found in the precise modelling of numerous outstanding individuals. NLP experts have discovered certain common themes that are driving the extraordinary achievements of these individuals by studying their habits and behaviors. They have distinctive strategies for motivating themselves and inspire others to achieve their goals. They are adept at creating deep relationships with others that are beneficial in positions such as Psychotherapy, management and sales. Additionally, they've achieved the art of resiliency by overcoming obstacles with unflinching determination, and using it to be the fuel to achieve unrivaled results. NLP provides people with the capability to turn challenges into potent motivators, similar to jet fuel, which propels them to their objectives.

But, NLP has the potential to transform even further than the amazing discoveries. NLP is, in its essence provides effective techniques to change behavior as well as personal growth. If giving a speech in front of a huge audience makes you feel nervous, NLP can change your perception and allow you to grow to a person who is comfortable with public speaking. NLP can alter your thinking so that you can enjoy the excitement of speaking public in large numbers as well as accelerating your need to be a part of even bigger audiences.

Richard Bandler and John Grinder invented John Grinder, Richard Bandler and Neuro-Linguistic Programming (NLP) in the 1970s in the beginning. Richard Bandler studied mathematics and computer sciences within the University of California, Santa Cruz. John Grinder was a linguistics teacher at the same institution.

Bandler and Grinder began their collaboration when each attended an Gestalt therapy class conducted by Fritz Perls, the founder of Gestalt therapy. Perls methods of therapy and their effects on the participants fascinated the pair. Inspired by Perls effectiveness of his methods, Bandler and Grinder set up to study and understand the qualities of excellence demonstrated by highly effective Therapists.

They started studying not just Fritz Perls, but also the family therapist Virginia Satir and renowned psychiatrist and psychotherapist Milton H. Erickson. Bandler and Grinder meticulously studied and analysed the language patterns used by therapists as well as nonverbal signals and techniques for therapeutic use.

Bandler and Grinder observed common patterns of behavior, communication as well as thought patterns that they believed to be responsible for the success of therapists in their work with clients, based on their analysis and observations. In order to establish the fundamental theories of NLP they fused theories from different disciplines, such as linguistics cybernetics and cognitive psychology as well as family systems theory.

The first of their books, "The Structure of Magic," released in 1975, introduced the patterns of language and techniques for therapeutic use they come across by using Perls as well as Satir modeling. It attracted a lot of interest and set the foundations for the expansion of NLP as a distinct discipline.

When NLP gained popularity and powerhouse individuals became involved in its creation and development. Robert Dilts was one such individual who significantly contributed to the growth of NLP and its application. Dilts was instrumental in the creation of the NLP method "Neurological Levels" and contributed to the research of values, beliefs and systems-thinking.

NLP is evolving since its creation as a number of practitioners as well as trainers have contributed to its development and adaption. A variety of other professionals as well as contributors from all kinds of disciplines have integrated NLP methods and principles in their research, expanding its application in therapies communications, coaching, education, business as well as personal growth.

The power of NLP extends beyond altering the way we think or perform things. It helps to understand the mechanism of the ways to transform. NLP serves as a guide, helping people along their journey to transformation. Though modeling is the main technique, NLP encourages practitioners to break out of the norm and set off into a new adventure of exploration and discovery. The training provides the foundation to develop powerful methods, however NLP creates an atmosphere of exploration and curiosity, encouraging users to venture into uncharted territories of self-improvement.

A willingness to be curious is the key to the development of your personal and professional skills Each new obstacle offers the chance to progress in the direction of greater mastery. Every client is a guide in the pursuit of your personal development and achievement.

NLP creates an incredibly strong curiosity in the minds of individuals which prompts them to ask questions the world around them, to explore, and uncover the secrets of their abilities. When the process progresses it is the desire to try new things that is a key ingredient to success.

Aiming to produce amazing results is at the heart of the NLP concept. Practitioners are able to weave the power of NLP throughout their living if they are equipped with the skills, knowledge and a constant determination to achieve. NLP helps people increase their abilities, improve their capabilities, and tap the reservoirs of their resilience. It's a transformational journey where the limits of personal growth can only be determined by the aspirations of one's imagination.

A well-known fable that has been told in NLP education programs across the globe over the past 40 years. A wise and old man was across the desert while returning return from a vacation by camel to an isolated village in the evening. Dehydrated and exhausted He pleaded for the water of one of the villager they immediately agreed and filled the thirst of his. Being in debt, the man wanted to know if there was something that he could do to repay the villager who showed him so much kindness.

"Actually, yes," was the reply of the villager walking towards the camel. "We are having a bit of an issue we'd prefer to have another opinion. In the present I'm the youngest of three boys and my father just died. The only thing he left us were 17 camels. His will decided that half of the herd would go to my brother who was the eldest and one third of it for my younger brother and the ninth went to me. What is the best way to divide 17 horses? I hope we don't need to cut down the camels."

The man contemplated for a while before declaring, "Please take me to your house." The man arrived at the residence and observed the two elder brothers screaming at each other in front of an open flame. The younger brother explained what was happening to the mediator, who declared, "Gentlemen, I have an answer. I would like to give you my camel for a gift. There are now 18 camels. Nine go to the elder brother. Six will be given towards the middle brother. Two will then take my friend to the next."

"Mister, mister! Only 17 camels are allotted, but there's an extra camel ..."; "Yes, and if you would possibly gift this camel back to me, I shall be on my way." Three brothers were grateful. three brothers were grateful to return the camel back to the owner.

The fundamental idea behind it is that Neuro Linguistic Programming ("NLP") seeks to mimic what a human does. For many chemical reactions, catalysts are used to increase the speed of reactions. This means that the catalysts help the reaction work generally, and aren't used up by the reactions. In the same way, the man made changes to that system, which was comprised of three brothers, and ultimately improving the efficiency of the entire system. Then the man gets his camel, which is his catalyst, back to ride out into the sunset not leaving any footprint.

NLP shows the endless capabilities of human talent. It's a beacon of hope for people seeking to achieve their goals in spite of the limitations they face. Your journey to self-discovery and self-discovery becomes a thrilling journey using NLP as a guide and the search for greatness is a never-ending potential horizon. If you accept the spirit of NLP and take it seriously, you'll be in the midst of a real adventure which will take you to endless potential of your brilliance.

What is the meaning of "neuro Linguistic programming"

Neuro refers to the neuronal system that includes our nervous system, brain and our sensoriality. The term is used to describe the concept that the experiences we experience undergo processing and representation in our brain system.

Linguistics: Treats language as well as other communication systems that are nonverbal. Language (words, idioms, titles, etc.) along with other forms that communicate nonverbally (gestures or signs etc.).) are a major factor in influencing our thinking decisions and behaviors. They are the primary factor in shaping our thinking and actions. languages in shaping our perceptions as well as our thoughts and actions. In both conscious and unconscious ways the way we speak and think has an impact in our ability to understand and understand our world.

Programming refers to programming language used in computers and means that we could "program" or change our behaviour patterns in order to get our desired outcomes. This implies that we can alter the way we behave and perform (automatically or in a routine manner) and enhance our interaction with other people by understanding and altering our thought habits and patterns of speech. It is essentially, the notion"programming "programming" implies having the ability to alter our behavior patterns to obtain desired outcomes.

So, examined as a whole NLP, when taken as a whole (NLP) suggests that we improve the quality of our thinking, skills and communication skills, emotional resilience as well as overall wellbeing by developing an awareness of unconscious patterns as well as leveraging the interactions of our words, thoughts and our actions.

It is possible that certifications for NLP are invalid. NLP certifications

There are a myriad of reasons why the possible invalidity of NLP certifications is an area of concern for members of the NLP community, especially within the United States. Even though NLP remains an effective method for personal development as well as communication, the absence an internationally-standardized certification system can cause some certifications be challenged. These are the primary reasons NLP certifications might not be valid:

The lack of standardization is a major issue. Unlike other professions that have universally accepted accreditation boards and standards, NLP does not have an internationally recognized standard for certification. Trainers from different organizations could have their own programs for certification and this can lead to differences in qualifications for training and assessments.

The court battle among NLP Co-Founders Richard Bandler and John Grinder caused concern about the ownership rights of NLP methods and the certifications. The verdict of the suit has declared NLP as being in the public domain which undermines the claim of exclusivity. The result was a heightened uncertainty about the authenticity in the validity NLP certifications.

Certification Mills: As a result of the inability to standardize methods for certification, several certification mills have appeared with the aim of providing NLP certifications that have no requirement for training. There have been questions regarding the legitimacy and validity of certain NLP certifications.

Uncontrolled oversight: As there isn't a centrally-controlled regulator or governing body that oversees NLP certifications, responsibility for the standards and contents of NLP courses is a bit shaky. Due to the absence of supervision, NLP certified professionals could have differing degrees of proficiency.

Unconformity in Training Quality Content, quality and length of NLP certifications can differ significantly. There are some programs that do not provide an adequate amount of training and assessment which results in professionals with inadequate skills and understanding.

Diverse NLP trainers might use distinct approaches and strategies and methods, which could result in conflicting advice and approaches in members of the NLP community. A lack of consistency may cause uncertainty and doubt regarding the effectiveness of NLP.

The perception and skepticism are due to the absence of standard procedures for certification and the historical controversy regarding NLP Certain experts, as well as those in other disciplines are skeptical about NLP certifications.

In addition to any other aspect that the litigation between Bandler and Grinder created major challenges to the discipline of Neuro-Linguistic Programming (NLP) in the early 1990s. The dispute over legal rights with Richard Bandler and John Grinder the co-founders and founders of NLP has had profound implications regarding NLP accreditation and the practitioners. Although NLP was thriving globally however, the impact of this case continues to affect NLP methods across America. United States.

Richard Bandler filed a multimillion-dollar lawsuit against John Grinder and others in 1996. Richard Bandler claimed that he was the sole owner of the Society of NLP. The suit had a significant influence on NLP accreditation processes and led to confusion between trainers and NLP practitioners. The consequences of the suit could be felt across the NLP community across the United States. Trainers were unsure regarding NLP certification and many weren't able to distinguish themselves from normal NLP methods due to the legal complications. At the Visionary Leadership conference in Santa Cruz, California, the litigation became the most talked about topic for NLP trainers from all over the globe. John Grinder sought support for his legal defence and Richard Bandler's lawyer addressed the conference. The trial lasted for nine days that ended at the end of February. Court rulings concluded that the claims made by Bandler of exclusivity ownership of the NLP were not substantiated as well as the court declared NLP to be part of the domain of public interest. The case highlighted the inexistence of a single worldwide standards to be used for NLP certification. The fear and anxiety faced by NLP practitioners across the United States following the court's ruling. A lot of NLP instructors have changed their names, or removed themselves from NLP certification. The United States, there is not a universally accepted NLP certification standards.

The case of Bandler-Grinder is a pivotal event in the history of NLP and influenced certification procedures and the trust of professionals. Despite the negative impact of the litigation, NLP thrived globally as a highly effective instrument for professional development and excellence in communication. In the present, NLP practitioners all over the globe embrace its transformational power, while also navigating various certification procedures and guidelines.

What's the Unconscious Mind?

The subconscious mind is an expansive and mysterious landscape which houses the entirety of our unconscious emotions, thoughts and sensations. A few aspects of this world are easy to draw our notice. Stop for a second and pay attention to the sound all around you. Sounds that you were at first unaware of, but now are. Similar to this, some behavior patterns like fidgeting can occur with no conscious consciousness, however when they are they are brought to our attention we are able to be affected by them and take control of these behaviors.

With the holistic method of NLP that is a holistic approach to NLP, the lines between the mind's unconscious as well as the body's physical systems, for instance the complex electrical impulses that drive our heartbeat and chemical reactions that control the heartbeat, are blurred. Instead of being distinct entities defined by lines of rigidity, the mind and body interact and form one interconnected unit. This perspective can empower people as it is a recognition that mind-body interaction can produce amazing effects on body which is supported by many studies. NLP is a broad range of patterns. It is beyond what one could ever require to become a skilled practitioner that can control the state of one's being, as well as tackling issues like allergies. It is a reminder that the entirety of our lives are connected, which allows the user to profit from the connectivity.

It is crucial to understand the fact that NLP insists on "influence," rather than total control of the bodily functions. Although NLP offers a way towards growth and improvement, it doesn't mean that you have total control over the entirety of the bodily processes. NLP is a continuous process that offers a variety of opportunities to develop and improve its strategies throughout the course of our life. Some individuals may apply NLP concepts to the extreme which can lead to assertions like avoiding using the term "growth" in discussions about your personal growth to prevent cancer. These ideas are undoubtedly exaggerated, and they miss the core of the purpose behind NLP.

Language is an effective instrument in NLP since the subtle choices we make in words are able to have a significant influence on how we perform and the results. While learning NLP and develop your skills, you'll encounter strong language patterns that can aid you as you work to build the necessary skills to lead better living. The unconscious brain plays an important role in deciding what is brought into our consciousness, what we are able to do without conscious thought or not, and also what our mind filters block. Neuroscientists have also identified certain areas of the brain that are devoted to removing sensations that allow us to concentrate on crucial activities while identifying the possibility of danger.

The unconscious mind manages many tasks, elements of our behaviour which we don't consciously take into consideration influence an enormous part of our actions. This fact entitles us to an immense responsibility that is similar to an art since the mind of our unconscious has the ability to influence our behavior negatively. The way we behave is subtly controlled without conscious thought similar to how experienced animal trainers influence the behaviors of tigers dolphins and dogs. The experiences we have, our temperaments as well as commercial advertising programs influence our minds, and can result in psychological defences that block us from self-awareness. When this happens, NLP acts as an solution, giving us techniques to alter our behaviors in line with our values and helping us to become self-aware in the areas that are most required.

NLP can be used to liberate individuals from their self-imposed limits and allow them to become active and assertive within their lives, and set off in a positive direction towards actions. Stress decreases because the subconscious mind lets go of the necessity to constantly defend itself and individuals reconnect to their joys, passions and the higher ideals. This shift in mindset enhances their success overall as well as their attractiveness. It opens up the doors to opportunities and opportunities for inspiration.

Chapter 10: What Is The Level Of Education?

The learning levels of NLP assist us to comprehend the progress of skills development and proficiency for any skill or subject. The levels are:

1. Unconscious Incompetence: Someone is not yet competent in a particular area or skill but is not aware of their incompetence or lack of capability. They're completely ignorant of the significance of this skill.

Someone who has not had a chance to play a musical instrument isn't aware of the significance of learning one

2. Concious Lack of Competence: During this point an individual is aware of their ignorance or incompetence and realizes that they necessity to improve and learn on this subject. They are keen to acquire how to master the art.

Anyone who is aware that they're in need of improving their public speaking ability and chooses to get instruction is an example.

3. Conscious Competence: A person has developed the abilities and know-how, however they need to be able to focus on and use their skills to be able to perform the task. It requires focus and effort.

Consider, for instance, the new driver that must be attentive to the mirrors, road as well as other drivers when driving.

4. Unconscious Competence: A person is able to practice the technique so many times that it's nearly unconsciously performed and takes little effort. They are able to perform the task without thinking about it since it is a routine.

A skilled pianist For instance, a skilled pianist can play complicated pieces of music without needing to look up the music sheet or think about the placement of fingers.

5. The art of mastery (Conscious or unconscious) is the top level of education is mastery. In this stage an individual is not able to just perform the task easily, but also be able to adapt and experiment with creativity. They've learned the technique until they have the ability to think and innovate over the basics. For instance, a master chef is an example. They can make extraordinary and delicious dishes, by not following a recipe.

People can gauge the progress they have made and their growth across any subject or skill through understanding their learning level. This also helps them improve their planning of the course of their education, pinpoint areas that require more training or support as well as set achievable goals in order to make improvements. Learning levels are a way to aid individuals in adjusting the way they learn and, ultimately, master the field they choose, be it studying NLP or another discipline.

What's the congruity?

In NLP the term "congruence" refers to an harmonious and harmony in the individual wherein all components of their mind behaviours, motivations, and psyche collaborate. The alignment of these elements is crucial for the effectiveness and efficacy of NLP tools.

If our senses including auditory, visual, and kinesthetic, are all in tune, we are at the initial level of congruence. A misalignment of these three modalities may result in internal contradictions and hinder our ability react effectively to the world around us.

On a more general dimension, is about the harmony of our components and can be described as being similar to miniature personalities or groups of our motivations. If these parts work in harmony and complement one another and we experience a feeling of inner peace.

Additionally, it is at its peak when the alignment extends to the highest values and objectives. It is a feeling of deep satisfaction and content when our decisions, actions as well as goals align to our fundamental values.

The people who do not have congruity or lack congruity On the other hand they may display behaviors and words that don't match up with their goals. Examining incongruities with these people might reveal more underlying misalignments doubt about their objectives or unresolved fears.

Incompletely resolved mental health issues or neurological issues, apathy to personal problems, or conflicts between motives and desires are only some of the causes for inconsistency. NLP methods aim to aid people in solving these issues and to achieve reintegration in where their components are well-integrated and function in a harmonious way.

The ability to align is a crucial component of the NLP process for coaches as well as consultants who deal with clients with incongruence. NLP helps individuals achieve the highest level of personal performance and heal by solving inconsistencies and dealing with them. In the end, it is congruence that forms the basis on the basis of which NLP creates transformational personal growth and self-awareness.

What is the difference between objectivity and subjectivity?

Subjectivity as well as objectivity are the two primary NLP notions that address the way people perceive and interpret their experience.

The individual and unique view of an individual perceives and experiences the world around them is known as subjectivity. This includes thoughts, feelings about beliefs, thoughts, and reactions to external stimulus. Subjectivity is a key feature of NLP recognizes the distinctiveness of each individual's experience and the significance of their personal worldview that influences their experience.

In contrast the term "objectivity" refers to data which is verifiable and observable and can be attributed to multiple persons. explain. The basis of this is facts and evidence from the outside. The importance of objectivity is emphasized in NLP because of the importance in discerning between individual interpretations and the actual reality of events.

NLP recognizes that subjectivity as well as objectivity play an important role in shaping our perception about the universe. Personal experiences affect our understanding, whereas the objective information provides better, more tangible and coherent understanding of the world. NLP Practitioners, however know the dangers of using our language, and the impact it has on our perception.

NLP Practitioners rely on Alfred Korzybski's phrase the idea that "the map is not the territory," founded upon the general semantics. That means our mental representations of ourselves (the map) don't always accurately reflect the reality of our external surroundings (the the territory). Our personal filters, beliefs and prejudices affect our perceptions and beliefs, which could cause perceptions that are subjective.

NLP as well as general semantics stress the importance of understanding and using language to be a useful instrument. Although language is effective in communicating as well as expression, it may result in misunderstandings or miscommunications, which can lead to negative results. In the end, NLP will help people learn to be aware of their personal interpretations and to question their beliefs and work towards an understanding that is more precise of reality.

Subjectivity as well as objectivity are two of the most fundamental elements of NLP that draw the focus on an person's personal experience as well as the external world. The impact of language is on perception. NLP practitioners seek to employ words with care to attain better interpersonal communication, personal growth as well as excellence.

What are Subliminal Messages?

Subliminal is a term used to describe things that are not visible to the conscious mind It has the potential to affect us, even when we don't even know of their existence. However, there are numerous assumptions about subliminals. These originated from an advertising expert in the 1950s. He asserted that the flashing of pictures or phrases during an event could entice viewers into purchasing certain items. Even though he admitted later to making up these claims, scientists found that his techniques proved ineffective. The realm of subliminals and

NLP extends beyond that offering alternative strategies for harnessing the power of NLP.

Many methods may render something subliminal. For instance, fleeting sound or images that are far too brief to be recognizable by conscious awareness. NLP is a particular example. It employs subliminals that operate beneath the level of conscious awareness, influencing the behavior of a person through hidden words and speech that is invisible to the person's attention. These subliminal messages evade conscious awareness in either putting your attention away from the present or causing a state of trance that makes conscious perception restricted. Milton Erickson, a renowned psychotherapist, developed a variety of methods of subliminal communication, such as hidden commands that are cleverly concealed in sentences. In addition, unclear subliminals transmit hidden messages that evade the receiver's defenses while creating a lasting impression.

Subliminal messages, on contrary, do not have the powerful commanding force of the overt messages or complicated communications. The effects are different from classic subliminal recordings. They began to appear in the 1950s, and often did not deliver the results they promised. NLP On contrary, utilizes subliminals to aid in an overall strategy that emphasizes control of state for best outcomes. Subliminal influence can be compared to the distinction between the hardness and the color of an object. For instance, a coin is hard regardless of even if it's not being perceived in a conscious manner while color comes from the complicated interplay of light and brain's sensor processing.

NLP highlights the difference between effects and perception in its exploration of the realm of subconscious. While one might not be aware of certain events it is possible for them to influence your mental health. The same is true for the way that advertisers craft clever products into the television and film industry that leave an impression of subliminal nature in the mind of viewers regardless of their conscious attention. Subliminals, who are adept at triggering emotions or feelings, enhance the probability of inducing behaviour which is in line with those emotions. Psychological research has proven that secure priming like the expression "mommy and I are one," helps people be more secure and confident in their actions.

But subliminal messages also can be misused, since those who have control over their population may utilize techniques for priming to induce the fear of and anxiety. Prejudice-inducing actions and behaviors could be cultivated by focusing on the safe base, which can lead groups to back conflict or to discriminate against minorities. The exploitation strategy causes the hypervigilance of people, which makes them more at risk of being influenced by news reports which reveal the truth. Untruthful practices employed by news media that are geared towards increasing viewers contrast strongly with the principles of NLP that are geared towards fostering honesty and excellence throughout all areas of our lives.

Subliminals are, at their core, offer a form of control beyond our conscious consciousness in which subtle signals such as words, images, or even words create a permanent impression on our mind's landscape. NLP is a potent power for personal improvement and empowerment, makes use of subliminal signals to bring about positive change, connecting actions to inner motives and beliefs. This insightful journey to self-development and authentic living stands out against the dark manipulative practices of those who take advantage of the human mind for discriminatory goals. The journey begins on the path that leads to self-discovery and positive change without deceit and fear by accepting the moral and powerful fundamentals of NLP.

Chapter 11: What's A Representation?

The concept "representation" encompasses the fascinating method by which we see and store mental images of the world within our heads. Think about the simple task of contemplating chair. The mental image that is generated is different for each individual. One person might imagine a wood chair, whereas others might envision a cushioned chair of some specific shade. The images that are shared on this site are personal and only belong to the individual viewing.

If we are on the road to success and success, the significance of representation is increased. The representations we make of ourselves can be effective allies that propel us forward or formidable barriers that hinder our advancement. Through this program you'll learn valuable strategies for enhancing and improving the mental representations you use so they can be more suited towards your objectives and goals.

Our brains are not simply objects. They also convey abstract concepts and deep believed values. How these ideas depicted has an enormous influence on how we feel, our actions, and relationships with other people. When you go through the details of this course it will give you profound insight into how to shape your mind's depictions of values and ideas that will allow you to maximize your potential to be empowered and make a difference on the people in your life.

The interplay between our mental representations with our quest of perfection is a process that leads to self-discovery and empowerment. It is possible to change the way we see and perceive the world through fine-tuning and adjusting our perceptions, raising our awareness level, and creating a new world of possibilities. It is possible to navigate the complex mental landscape by using these powerful tools by creating images that encourage to motivate and inspire positive action that is in line to your highest dreams and goals.

Every person's unique perception of reality is a unique view of the world. Recognizing and enhancing these perceptions are the key to the way to achieve excellence. It is possible to explore a universe of infinite possibilities when you accept the transformational power of the mental image and create the path to success through the brilliance of your representations. Begin to explore this wonderful aspect of your thoughts and you'll realize the art of your mental images can be the essence of perfection.

What's a Representational System?

Rep systems, sometimes referred to as sense modalities, play an crucial in the way we see and interpret information of our environment. Five primary senses include visually (seeing) as well as auditory (hearing) as well as tactile (feeling/touching) as well as gustatory (tasting) as well as the sense of olfaction (smelling). Recognizing and utilizing rep systems could result in profound changes in how people react to different situations. It could be helpful in attaining the highest level of excellence.

The auditory, visual and kinesthetic systems comprise the three major rep system. Visual rep is distinguished by thinking through images and visualization in the mind. It also is based on the perception of sight. Auditory rep is built upon hearing and deals in processing information using the sounds of language and patterns. The rep system of kinesthetics is involved with bodily sensations and feelings and is vital for emotional experience.

In addition to the usual senses, two additional rep systems are essential in understanding how experiences are stored and then recovered. The gustatory rep system deals with taste while the Olfactory rep system deals with the sense of smell.

Digital auditory rep system as well as the most popular rep system however are among the top aspects of rep systems.

This system of auditory digital representation is focused on our communication with each other using the language that we utilize to think, as well as the way we think about information. The way in which we interact with ourselves using the digital auditory system could provide a significant personal development instrument.

The primary sense system that an individual rely on the most is often called the most preferred rep system. Understanding which rep system is preferred by a particular person helps improve communications and connections. Additionally, it allows the creation of more efficient methods and strategies that are aligned with the rep's preferred system. This results in more effective outcomes.

Rep systems are beneficial since they provide the basis for recording as well as retrieving the experiences we have. They provide the base of our thinking, actions as well as our memories. Marketing and advertising professionals acknowledge the value of rep systems and use these systems to alter consumer behavior through the creation of commercials and other products that trigger certain sensory reactions.

As every step and decision-making process relies on an order and choosing of rep systems, knowing rep systems can lead to deeper analysis of the strategies. Understanding the rep system of individuals who are successful can offer important insights and secrets. In the same way, knowing someone's primary rep structure can be crucial element to providing efficient assistance and assistance.

The ability to understand and use rep systems could influence the way we interact with others and how we influence them.

Rep systems, sometimes referred to as sense modalities are the five senses that we use to perceive and process information. They include visually (seeing) as well as auditory (hearing) and the kinesthetic (feeling/touching) as well as gustatory (tasting) and the olfactory (smelling). Two additional important rep systems: the auditory digital, that is our language to think and our thoughts, and the more popular rep system that is the predominant sense that one relies on most.

It is essential to recognize an individual's rep system for efficient communication and connections. Rep systems of people are often identified by the language they speak. Most likely, they are using an image rep method whenever they speak about the way things appear or what they observed or what colours. Most likely, they are using the auditory rep system when they focus on the sounds they hear. This could be the sounds they hear or auditory clues. It is likely that they use their kinesthetic rep system when they speak about emotions emotion, intuitions.

To influence and build relationships with other people, we should adapt our messages to the preferred method of communication. If, for instance, one relies heavily on their visual senses, it is important to use imagery as well as visual clues. The message should be geared towards someone's feelings and emotions in the event that they are more tactilely inclined.

Rep systems focus on the internal experience and beliefs and external perceptions. Involving both external and internal aspects could have a more profound effect on the individual. Attracting a person's inner beliefs and motivations, for instance, could be more convincing than evidence from outside.

The body language is an effective way of connecting and appealing to a person's rep system. It is possible to establish confidence and rapport by mimicking their rep style through gestures and body language. In the case of someone who emphasizes their auditory system it is possible to use subtle gestures of listening or lean back by turning our ear towards the person.

It's crucial to recognize that rep systems used by people may change depending on the subject or the context of the discussion. The ability to adapt to various rep systems is crucial for successful communications.

What's VAK?

The three main sensory modes that we use to perceive and manage information are described as VAK. They are the visual (seeing) and auditory (hearing) and the kinesthetic (feeling). Knowing and using these methods not only helps strengthen relationships with people around us, but also opens the door to the creation of efficient strategies to excel.

Practitioners of NLP acknowledge the immense effect of VAK to shape our experience and our interactions. They can customize their approach to communication to more deeply resonate with the individual's preferred method of interpreting the world. It is achieved through observing the person's primary sensory preferences. The increased understanding and rapport provide a strong basis for building connections and encouraging personal development.

When educators explore the world of VAK and gain insight into how they can improve the educational experiences of their students. The educators can create teaching methods that accommodate different types of learning by understanding the fact that all students can be benefited by focusing on a particular sensory method over others. Visual learners, for instance, can be benefited by visual aids, diagrams and drawings, while an auditory student could benefit from explaining things verbally and discussion. In the same way, learners who are kinesthetic are benefited by hands-on learning and hands-on learning.

Utilizing VAK techniques in education is proven to increase the student's engagement, comprehension and retention. Utilizing multi-sensory methods makes sure that students aren't only limited to one mode of processing information, creating the development of a multi-sensory and integrated learning setting.

Studies in cognitive and educational psychology is continuing to confirm the concept that adapting to various learning styles enhances performance in learning. Researchers such as Howard Gardner's theories of multiple intelligences highlight the importance of acknowledging and respecting various types of sensory processing and intelligence.

What are the Eye Accessing Cues (EAC)?

Eye-accessing signals, also referred to as eye movements or patterns, are non-verbal signals that may reveal crucial data about how an individual perceives information and interacts with different sensory modes. Eye movements are believed to be associated with certain types of rep and thinking systems in accordance with the theories that underlie Neuro-Linguistic Programming (NLP)

The concept behind these signals is that whenever people are thinking or remembering details, their eyes are moved with specific patterns that are based on the type of sensory mode they're employing. These signals can tell if the person is able to access their memories and thoughts through the auditory, visual or tactile sensors.

A brief summary of cues for eye access:

Visual (V) looking up and left (from the perspective of their eyes) can be associated with seeing visual images, creativity as well as memories of previous occasions. When you request someone for a memory of an unforgettable vacation spot they could look upwards and then to the left, thinking about the place.

Auditory (A) Horizontal gaze towards the left (from one's point of view) can be associated with the ability to access auditory information like recollecting conversation, sounds or internal dialogue. When they are asked to recall a favourite song, for instance you might look from a horizontal position towards the left, while "hearing" the melody.

Kinesthetic (K) The act of looking towards the left and down (from your point of view) can be associated with the feeling of emotions, feelings, as well as body feelings. If asked about their most memorable memories, for instance, they could look to the left and down towards the left and connect to their emotional experiences.

Auditory Digital (AD): The horizontal view to the left (from the perspective of their eyes) can be a sign of the ability to access internal dialogue, analytical thinking and self-talk. This is the method that we employ when thinking about ourselves.

It is vital to understand that cues to access the eyes are not always correct, and different people might make different eye movements depending upon factors like the culture of their origin, personal preferences as well as the type of the information processing. Additionally, certain people might not display distinct eye movements or utilize a mix of signals.

Therefore these eye-accessing cues should serve as a guide instead of a conclusive indication of someone's thinking decision-making process. Knowing these cues could help you better understand how other people process information as well as build better communication and relationship with the people you interact with. For a better knowledge of the person's thinking and emotions, think about the context of their words and mix the context with other types of communication. It's the same with all nonverbal signals.

It is true the fact that not everyone's brains are brain-wired in the same way with regards to eye-access signals. Many people display the normal eye movements attributed to particular rep systems, as explained in NLP There are certain exceptions and nuances between different individuals.

A few people could experience reversed eye-accessing cues meaning that the movements of their eyes differ from what most viewers see. According to NLP researchers, people with left hands as well as those who have cerebral hemispheres that function in the opposite direction could display reversed eye-accessing signals. Someone who is left handed, for example, might be able to access information visual by turning their eyes horizontally towards the left instead of to right.

Additionally, certain people might show very subtle or even slight eye movements. This makes it harder to discern the rep systems they use most often via eye-accessing cues. To comprehend their thoughts and their preferred rep system you must observe more closely and search at other signals that are nonverbal as well as communication patterns.

In addition, certain individuals may be more erratic or mixed eye movements that can be a result of various factors for instance, neurological disorders or emotional disturbance. When this happens it is crucial to treat the individual without judging them and not make presumptions solely based on their eyes movement.

Additionally, certain people might use a rep system does not use or are not using. It could be due to individual preferences, past events, or other emotional issues. If this is the case, communicating via predicates relating to that specific rep system could not be effective or appropriate.

As a matter of fact, in terms of an "lead rep system," certain people might prefer to connect to a certain rep system when they are taking notes or participating in conversations. It doesn't mean that they use it as their first or their preferred rep system. It is simply their rep system that they utilized in the beginning. In the course of conversation it is possible that they will gain access to other rep systems.

Although eye-accessing cues give valuable insight into the way an individual processes data, it's crucial to realize that people's eyes and their preferences for rep systems can be different. Understanding these differences in addition to using these cues to serve as a reference rather than the sole rule could aid in better comprehension and interaction with others.

Chapter 12: What Are The Predicates?

Predicates are the words or phrases which indicate the person's preference for a sensory system, or the representational system when they communicate in the setting in the context of Neuro-Linguistic Programming (NLP). According to NLP that people process and interpret their experiences by using three primary sensory modes that are also known as VAK: Visual Kinesthetic, and Auditory.

1. Visual predicates are the words or phrases that indicate a person's preference for the visual system. Visual predicates can refer to words such as "see, look, show, imagine, picture, view," and others. The majority of people who use visual predicates typically interpret information and convey their thoughts through visual imagery as well as visual signals.

In this case, "I see what you mean." "Can you show me how to do it?"

2. Auditory predicates. These are the words or phrases which indicate the individual's preference for the hearing sensor. Auditory predicates refer to terms that relate to hearing, for example "hear, listen, sounds, tell, talk," and others. People who utilize auditory predicates often process information through audio-visual cues, inner dialogue as well as sounds.

"That sounds great!" as an example. "Let's have a talk about it."

3. Kinesthetic predicates are the words or phrases that express a person's preference to the kinesthetic sensor. These are words related to touch feelings, emotions and physical sensations such as "feel, touch, grasp, get a handle on, gut feeling," are instances of kinesthetic predicates. The majority of users who use kinesthetic predicates depend on their feelings as well as bodily sensations in order to comprehend and express their feelings.

"I'm excited about the opportunity," to take an instance. "I have a feeling something isn't right."

NLP recognizes two other minor predicates along with these three primary predicates:

4. Gustatory predicates: Words that refer to taste or phrases, such as "taste, savor, delicious," and others. They are not as commonplace used in daily conversation.

"This idea has a funky taste," as an example.

5. Olfactory predicates: words that are related to scents or phrases like "smell, scent, aroma," and others. They're also not as often employed in daily conversation.

In this case, "This smells like a fishy business."

The ability to identify a person's predicates could give valuable insight into how they perceive information and the world. NLP practitioners aim to build relations and build relationships with other people by reflecting and matching their predicates when communicating. Knowing the dominant sensory system may also aid in adjusting communication and learning strategies to the individual's preference and style of learning.

What exactly are dissociation and associations?

They penetrate into the unconscious which influences how we interact with ourselves and our outer world.

Dissociation, in essence, refers to the state of being disconnected from the normal state of consciousness as well as our core. The mind seems to withdraw from ourselves and create the impression that we are detached. The phenomenon could serve as an effective defense mechanism that provides some relief from the discomfort as well as a sense of objectivity in dealing with situations when dealing with difficult issues NLP experience. Dissociation that is controlled lets people explore their own thoughts and emotions in a detached manner and allows them to develop an comprehension of their own reactions and responses.

The concept of association, on contrary, is an unwavering connection to our experience. It is about being conscious of our feelings, thoughts and feelings, and taking a deep dive into the experience of the moment. It is an "first-hand" experience in which you are fully engaged and engaged in the course of things. The process of association allows us to feel the emotion of our feelings and to see things from an extremely subjective viewpoint.

But it's crucial to realize that certain sufferers may be struggling to manage their feelings of dissociation because of factors like brain injuries or trauma. When this happens there is an increased sense of disconnection as if they are navigating fog. The fragmentation of their self could hinder the smooth function of the various parts of their personalities, resulting in disarray and disorientation. In order to create a strong and integrated sense of self-awareness, NLP recognizes the importance of maintaining a balance between dissociation and associations. Different NLP techniques are designed to help people integrate the various aspects of their personality and thereby enabling them to be a harmonious power. NLP helps to create a more comprehensive and unified sense of self-awareness and comprehension by bridges the gaps between diverse aspects of the personality.

In the real world, associations and dissociation are valuable techniques to be found in the NLP toolbox. The people who employ these state appropriately can gain greater insight into their thoughts, feelings and reactions, which can lead to personal transformation and growth. It is important to know the right time to engage in association for a deeper experience of emotions, and also when it is appropriate to disconnect to get an broader view and keep an objective perspective. In addition, the interactions between the two processes provides a deep insights into our mental and emotional process. NLP Practitioners use this information to assist their clients in navigating complicated issues, enhance self-awareness, as well as effect significant shifts in perception and behavior.

What is sub-modality?

Sub-modalities are the nitty gritty distinctions and the building blocks of every representational system. This comprises five senses: auditory, visual and kinesthetic. They also include gustatory and the olfactory. They play a crucial role in the way we experience and store our memories our thoughts, feelings, and thoughts.

We will investigate sub-modalities by using every one of the representational systems:

1. Sub-modalities of the rep visual system relate to certain aspects of vision experience. When you're asked to picture trees, for instance it is possible to examine the clarity of the picture (clear or blurred) as well as its the brightness (bright or dim) as well as color intensity (vivid as well as dull).

2. Sub-modalities of the auditory system: Sub-modalities that are part of the auditory rep system relate to different characteristics of sound or auditory experiences. If you're asked to listen for the birds that are in the tree it is possible to detect quality of the sound, its quality (clear as well as muffled) and frequency (high and low) and emotional impact (soothing or annoying).

3. Sub-modalities within the kinesthetic rep system relate to the emotions and sensations that accompany the experience. When you're asked how you react towards the birds and tree there are a variety of emotions like ease or tension, warmth and even the blushing. Feelings like joy, sadness

or anxiety are created by the combination of these feelings.

It is important to note that sub-modalities do not have to be limited to one representational system. Different modalities may share sub-modalities. As an example, when somebody says that the colors are "loud," they are speaking about the strength and the brightness of the colors and not the sounds. Similar to when an audio is called "sharp," it has the appearance of being irritated or edgy.

Knowing sub-modalities is useful in the development of your personal as well as communication. It is possible to alter how we react and perceive events by understanding as well as manipulating the sub-modalities. NLP practitioners typically employ sub-modalities to assist people in changing the way they react to certain situations, for example changing negative feelings into positive ones or changing their limiting belief systems into more positive ones. The individual can have greater control over their emotions and thoughts and create positive change in their lives through the use of sub-modalities.

The difference between sub-modalities analog and digital is determined by how data is represented by the respective representational systems (modality).

1. Analogue Submodalities Sub-modalities are constant and may be increased or decreased without altering the quality of sensory experiences. They are flexible and adaptable. For the visual mode such as the clarity of images, their brightness as well as color saturation represent analog sub-modalities. These attributes can be altered but still keep the image identifiable as meaningful. Similar to the volume or pitch as well as the emotional impact of sound are sub-modalities of analog in the auditory mode.

2. Digital Sub-modalities Digital sub-modalities however are discrete, and employ recognized symbols or particular elements to convey the information. They tend to have fixed perceptions, and they are not as adaptable. Words for instance are digital sub-modalities of the auditory digital mode. Written language, like words written on a paper, is a sub-modality digital of representation in visual form. The symbols are associated with particular meanings, and can't be scaled easily up or down, without altering the meaning or meaning.

The difference between analog and digital sub-modalities can have practical implications regarding communication, and the way people make sense of information. Since digital sub-modalities are less rigid, they are much more easily altered or destroyed. Altering the order of sentences can drastically alter the meaning of. Analogue sub-modalities on the contrary, can allow greater subtle variations, without sacrificing the core of what you are experiencing.

The understanding of the role of analog and digital sub-modalities of NLP can be useful in influence and communication. The choice of the correct digital sub-modalities (specific terms and symbols) to craft a compelling message for instance, could have an effect on the clarity of the message and its significance. Analog sub-modalities are a great way to trigger emotions, or even create visuals that stimulate positive changes of behavior and perception.

People can develop their communication skills as well as comprehend the way they process information across diverse sensory forms by knowing as well as working with analog and digital sub-modalities.

The visual sub-modalities Worksheet (worksheet #264 in The book "500 Practical NLP Forms, Templates & Worksheets"):

Feel the power of sub-modalities

Let's begin with an exercise which will show us how our minds function with sub-modalities! Sub-modalities are the basis for our thinking and feelings. They impact how we think and retain information.

Think about a memory that's not too thrilling or upset, but instead neutral or at least mildly enjoyable. Did you remember it? Close your eyes and think of the memories.

Note what's happening in the memory now. What is it that you can notice? Are you seeing either dark or light? Colourful or monochrome? Do you think it's close, to say just in front of you or distant or far off?

Pay attention to the sounds that are in the memory. Are they soft or hard? Are they loud or clear? Take note of specifics.

Then, you can feel the feelings or sensations that are associated to this particular memories. What part of your body do you feel these sensations? Are you feeling a warm sensation on your chest or within your fingers?

Try these sub-modalities right now! Try increasing the brightness or dimension of the image like increasing brightness and saturation of a TV. What impact does this have on the way you feel about memories?

Try the reverse. Dim the brightness and dimension of the picture. Note any changes in your emotions.

Let's start listening to the sound. You can turn up the volume on your radio, making the sound clearer and more loud. What impact does this has in your experience of memory?

Try to make the sound more muffled and soft now. Check to see if this alters your thoughts about the memories.

Let's try our hand at the emotions. Transmit the feelings into another part in your body. What happens to your emotional reactions?

Modify the intensity, or speed of your mood. Consider how this affects your memory overall.

Aren't you intrigued? It is possible to alter how you perceive memories by altering the sub-modalities. This is almost like you had your own personal editing studio!

Take a look at a particular positive memories. It's something that makes you feel happy or exuberant. Did you get it? We can improve your memory!

Enhance the colors of your image to make them clearer and vivid. Make the sound to make them more enjoyable and rich.

The positive emotions that you feel will be reflected through your body in the warmth of a hug. Spend a few moments to be grateful for the magnificence of this moment.

Aren't you amazed at how the brain works? Sub-modalities affect our emotions and perception in a significant way. Through practice, you will be able to use this information to enhance the quality of your negative and positive experiences.

If you encounter a challenging moment or memory, keep in mind this routine. Try the sub-modalities and discover how they could transform your outlook and make the mental film better!

What's the meaning of anchors?

In the world of NLP An anchor can be an extremely effective method of accessing and invoking a particular mindset with a goal. While the word may bring thoughts of boats that are moored in tranquil harbors, anchors hold an even more significant significance for NLP. Anchors are the process of combining the use of a symbol, for example touching or gesture, with an desired emotional psychological state. A strong symbol, for instance an exact hand gesture or finger's position, could effortlessly trigger a mental state.

As an example, if you are able to associate the feeling of being confident by doing an "okay" sign with your non-dominant hand. Repeating this sign can allow you to be more comfortable. The process is referred to as activating your desired mental state with the selected image "firing the anchor." In this case the anchor is the means for getting access to and channeling our desired mental or emotional state that allows us to use it as needed.

Anchors, which are versatile NLP instruments, can be used for a wide range of situations. It is surprising that they are utilized unconsciously to affect the behavior of a person. Coaches for instance, might use an unfavorable anchor to discourage individuals from interfering in the process of healing. Grinder was one of the early pioneers of NLP has provided an original way of anchoring to the client with snake phobia as well as a tendency to distract herself in coaching sessions. Grinder was able to move his eyes to the floor and behind her, forming an anchor that was not conscious of her awareness.

Eye movement was an anchor. Each time Grinder activated it, the lady experienced discomfort. The discomfort then was related to her distracted behavior and resulted in her abrupt halt and subsequent decline in frequency. While she wasn't aware of the anchor's effects, their influence on her behavior was substantial.

Anchors, as such illustrate the depth and flexibility of the human mind. Utilizing anchors in a deliberate manner and in a conscious manner allows people to control their emotions as well as their reactions to various circumstances. People can tap into an immense pool of internal resources, and create an attitude which is in line with their objectives and goals by knowing and enhancing the power of these symbolic representations. It is possible to discover a stash of methods and strategies in the world of NLP that allow users to design and utilize anchors to help you achieve your personal growth and development.

It is possible to use the same techniques of anchoring you employ for yourself while instructing someone else. Anchors are able to be set up to serve specific purposes in coaching or even for temporary ones that could be beneficial. If, for instance, you're coaching a person who would like to become more assertive at work, but is struggling with the role of playing, you may play around with their the power of imagination.

Ask the client to think of times when they felt slightly confident and then to identify which part of their body which felt the most relaxed and expressive or more confident. Make a point in their left knee when they perform this. The repetition of this action could serve as an effective anchor.

Start with easy scenarios, like asking a colleague for their opinion to develop assertiveness. Start by firing the anchor, touching the left knee before they think about the situation. The client may be prompted to be more assertive. Pay attention to the sensation when they are more assertive, thereby enhancing the effectiveness of the anchor.

Another technique to use is fractionation. This requires focusing only on one specific mode at the moment. As an example, a person is able to watch their own situation while turning off the audio and listen to the scenario while turning off the picture. This can help make the practice more enjoyable for the participant.

www.ingramcontent.com/pod-product-compliance
Lightning Source LLC
Chambersburg PA
CBHW071445080526
44587CB00014B/1993